# *The* ABRAHAMIC PARADIGM

## *Pluralism, Salvation, and the Challenges of the Contemporary Abrahamic Trialogue*

## DR. ALI MOHAMED SALAH

LOOH PRESS
1446/2024

**LOOH PRESS LTD.**

Copyright © Ali Mohamed Salah 2024
First Edition, First Print *Jumād II* 1446/December 2024



For permission and requests, write to the publisher or the author, at the address below.

**PRINTED & DISTRIBUTED BY**

Looh Press Ltd.
56 Lethbridge Close
Leicester, LE1 2EB
England. UK
www.LoohPress.com
LoohPress@gmail.com

**CONTACT AUTHOR**

Ali.Kuantan@gmail.com

A catalogue record of this title is available from the British Library.

**COVER DESIGN & TYPESET**

Kusmin (Looh Press)

**ISBN**

978-82-693677-6-8.      (Paperback)

# TRANSLITERATION TABLE

(ء) = ’     (ا) = a / A / ā / Ā     (ب) = b / B

(ت) = t / T     (ث) = th / TH     (ج) = j / J

(ح) = ḥ / Ḥ     (خ) = kh / KH     (د) = d / D

(ذ) = dh / DH     (ر) = r / R     (ز) = z / Z

(س) = s / S     (ش) = sh / SH     (ص) = ṣ / Ṣ

(ض) = ḍ / Ḍ     (ط) = ṭ / Ṭ     (ظ) = ẓ / Ẓ

(ع) = ‘ / ʿ     (غ) = gh / GH     (ف) = f / F

(ق) = q / Q     (ك) = k / K     (ل) = l / L

(م) = m / M     (ن) = n / N     (ه) = h / H

(و) = w / W / ū / Ū     (ي) = y / Y / ī /

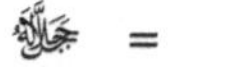 = Jalla Jallāluhu

= Subḥānahu Wa Taʿālā

= ‘Alayhis-Salām

= Sallalāhu ‘Alayhi Wasallam

= Raḥimahu Allāh

= Raḍiyallāhu ‘anhu

= Raḍiyallāhu ‘anhā

= Raḍiyallāhu ‘anhumā

بسم الله الرحمن الرحيم

*In the name of Allah,*
*the Most Gracious,*
*the Most Merciful*

ABRAHIMIC PRADIGM

**CONTENTS**


**DEDICATION** ............................................................ xiii

**ACKNOWLEDGEMENTS** ............................................. xv

**PREFACE** ................................................................. xvii

**PART 1:**
**PATHS OF TRUTH AND SALVATION IN THE ABRAHAMIC**
**RELIGIONS:** .............................................................01

1.1. Abstract ................................................................03

1.2. Foundational Overview of the Study:  Objectives, Motivation,
Challenges, Methodology, and Framework ....................... 07

Research Objectives ................................................... 07

Reasons for Choosing the Topic ................................. 08

Previous Studies: ....................................................... 08

Research Problem ...................................................... 08

Research Methodology ............................................... 09

Structure of the Research .......................................... 09

Research Methodology ............................................... 10

Structure of the Research .......................................... 10

1.3. Introduction ......................................................... 11

**1.0 ABRAHAMIC AFFILIATION IN SACRED TEXTS** .................. 13

1.1 The Religious Essence and Personality of Abraham in the Three
Sacred Scriptures ................................................... 13

1.2 His Missionary Efforts and Enduring Struggle ...................... 16

1.3 The message of Abraham (peace be upon him): ...................... 18

1.4 Abraham (Peace Be Upon Him)  and His Narrative in the Old
Testament ............................................................... 18

1.5 Abraham (Peace Be Upon Him) and His Narrative in the New
Testament ............................................................... 21

1.6 Abraham (Peace Be Upon Him) and His Faith in Qur'anic
Studies ................................................................... 22

1.7 The Truth of Abraham's Faith and His True Followers ......... 29

1.8 Unique Insights of the Qur'an Regarding Abraham (Peace Be
Upon Him): ............................................................ 30

1.9 Defining the Concept of Abrahamic Affiliation in Light of
Qur'anic Texts: ....................................................... 32

1.10 Insights Derived from the Verses: ............................. 33

1.11 Scriptural Perspectives on Abrahamic Affiliation: Raphael Patai's View ...................................................................................34

**2.0 RELIGIOUS PLURALISM WITHIN THE FRAMEWORK OF ABRAHAMIC AFFILIATION:  PERSPECTIVES AND POSITIONS** ...........................................................................................**35**

2.1 The Defining Characteristic of Abrahamic Affiliation: ...........35

2.2 The Concept of Religious Pluralism: .........................................37

2.3 Religious Exclusivism: ..............................................................37

2.4 Religious Inclusivism: ...............................................................39

2.5 Evidence Supporting Religious Inclusivism from the Three Abrahamic Religions ....................................................................40

2.5.1 In Judaism: .......................................................................40

2.5.2 In Christianity: .................................................................40

2.5.3 In Islam: ...........................................................................40

2.6 The Biblical View and Its Stance on Religious Pluralism: .......41

2.7 The First Islamic Perspective: ...................................................42

2.7.1 Exclusivity in the Path of Truth: .....................................43

2.7.2 Islamic Exclusivism: ........................................................43

2.7.3 Validity of Previous Messages: ........................................44

2.7.4 Quranic Evidence for Exclusivism: .................................44

2.7.8 Hick's Acknowledgment: .................................................45

2.8 The Second Islamic Perspective: ...............................................45

2.8.1 Religious Pluralism as a Quranic and Prophetic Principle: 45

2.8.2 The Universality and Multiplicity of Divine Messages... 45

2.8.3 Diversity as a Manifestation of Divine Mercy .................46

2.8.4 Islam as Submission to Allah ﷻ, Beyond Labels.............47

2.8.5 Freedom of Religion – "No Compulsion in Faith" ........47

2.8.6 Inclusivity in Quranic Verses on Religion......................48

2.8.7 The Three Criteria for Salvation......................................48

2.8.8 Historical Precedents of Coexistence .............................49

2.8.9 Conclusion: The Pluralistic Essence of Islam .................50

2.9 Discussion of these views: .........................................................51

2.10 Responses to the arguments presented by those supporting the idea of religious pluralism:..........................................................52

2.10.1 The "universality of divine messages" ...........................52

2.10.2 The "diversity of races, peoples, and colors" .................52

2.10.3 "Islam is referred to as the name for all divine religions". 53

2.10.4 The Qur'anic verse, "Let there be no compulsion in religion. ........................................................................ 53

2.10.5 "The Basic Conditions…" ................................................ 54

2.10.6 "Historical Evidence…" .................................................. 56

**3.0 CONCLUSION** ....................................................................... **59**

**4.0 RECOMMENDATIONS** ........................................................ **61**

**5.0 REFERENCES** ........................................................................ **63**

References in Arabic .................................................................... 63

Online sources .............................................................................. 64

References in English .................................................................. 64

**PART 2:**
**THE ABRAHAMIC DIALOGUE PROJECT BETWEEN JUDAISM, CHRISTIANITY, AND ISLAM:** ................................................... **65**

2.1. Abstract ................................................................................... 67

2.2. Foundational Overview of the Study: Objectives, Motivation, Challenges, Methodology, and Framework ............................. 71

Reasons for Choosing the Topic: .............................................. 71

The Problem Addressed by the Research: ................................ 73

Research Methodology: ............................................................... 73

Structure of the Research ........................................................... 74

2.3. Introduction ........................................................................... 75

**1.0 THE CHALLENGES AND CONCERNS SURROUNDING THE OBJECTIVES OF THE ABRAHAMIC DIALOGUE PROJECT** ....... **77**

1.1 Islamic Perspective on the Objectives of the Abrahamic Dialogue Project: ....................................................................... 78

1.1.1 Muslim Openness to Dialogue: ....................................... 78

1.1.2 Limits and Conditions for Dialogue: .............................. 78

1.1.3 The Philosophical Dimension of "Unity Among the Abrahamic Religions" ................................................................. 79

1.1.4 Compromising Religious Integrity: ................................. 79

1.1.5 Undermining the Finality of Islam: ................................ 80

1.1.6 Involving Participation in Their Worship and Religious Rituals: ........................................................................................... 81

**2.0 THE CHALLENGES TO ISLAMIC-JEWISH RECONCILIATION IN ACHIEVING THE ABRAHAMIC DIALOGUE PROJECT** ......... **85**

2.1 The Difficulties and Obstacles to Reconciliation Between the Followers of the Two Religions: ................................................ 86

2.1.1  The Ongoing Jewish Wars:................................................ 87

2.1.2 The Principle of Jewish Superiority and Racial
Distinction:................................................................. 89

2.1.3 The Jewish-Zionist Connection: A Complex Relationship
93

2.2 The Result of These Obstacles and the Proposed Solutions: ..96

**3.0 CHALLENGES TO ISLAMIC-CHRISTIAN CONVERGENCE IN REALIZING THE ABRAHAMIC DIALOGUE PROJECT................99**

3.1 Introduction to Islamic-Christian Relations: ........................99

3.2 Challenges and Obstacles to Islamic-Christian Convergence
within the Framework of the Abrahamic Project .................100

3.2.1 The Historical and Contemporary Political-Religious
Entanglements between East and West:....................... 101

3.3 Political and Religious Entanglements in the Past: .................101

3.4 Political Entanglement in the Present:...................................109

3.4.1 The Unipolarity of the Christian West, Its Sovereignty,
and Its View of Other Peoples:.................................. 113

3.4.2 The Christian West's Support for the Establishment of the
Zionist Entity in the Heart of the Islamic World: ....... 115

3.4.3 Attempts of Crusading Western Missionary Work through
Western Colonial Influence:........................................ 116

3.4.4 The Consequences of These Difficulties and the Proposed
Solutions: ............................................................... 117

3.5 The Position of Followers of Islam and Christianity on
Correcting Past Mistakes:.....................................................121

3.5.1 The Christian Perspective: ............................................ 121

3.5.2 The Islamic Perspective:................................................ 122

**4.0 CONCLUSION OF THE STUDY.....................................125**
**5.0 RECOMMENDATIONS...................................................127**
**6.0 REFERENCES.............................................................129**

References in Arabic...............................................................129

References in English.............................................................131

Online References..................................................................131

## DEDICATION

*I* dedicate this work to the blessed souls of my dearly beloved parents, whose unwavering love, sacrifices, and constant support have been a source of strength and guidance throughout my journey. May Allah ﷻ shower His boundless mercy upon them, grant them eternal peace, and reward them for their selfless devotion.

I also dedicate this book to the cherished memory of my esteemed PhD supervisor, Prof. Dr. Faisal H. Othman, may Allah ﷻ have mercy on him. His invaluable guidance, encouragement, and insight from 1996 to 2000 were instrumental in shaping the themes explored in this research. May Allah ﷻ grant him the highest ranks in Jannah, and reward him abundantly for his contributions to my academic journey and beyond.

Lastly, I dedicate this work to my family, whose unwavering love, encouragement, and belief in me have been my constant pillars. Their sacrifices and support have been a source of immense strength, and I am deeply grateful for their presence in my life. May Allah ﷻ bless and protect them always.

# ACKNOWLEDGEMENTS

I would like to express my heartfelt gratitude to my brothers, particularly Mohammed Isak Abdullahi, for their unwavering technical support throughout the process of bringing this work to its current form. Their invaluable contributions, guidance, and assistance have played an essential role in the successful completion and publication of this research. I am deeply appreciative of their dedication, efforts, and commitment, which have been indispensable to this endeavor. May Allah ﷻ reward them abundantly for their kindness and support.

## PREFACE

All praise is due to Allah ﷻ, the Almighty, and may His peace and blessings be upon His Messenger, Muhammad ﷺ.

It is with great humility and gratitude that I present these two writings, which are selected and refined versions of my PhD thesis titled *"The Abrahamic Interfaith Dialogue in View of the Qur'an."* This research was conducted between 1996 and 2000, during which I dedicated myself to exploring the intricate and multifaceted relationships among the Abrahamic faiths—Judaism, Christianity, and Islam—through the lens of the Qur'an. Over the years, I have expanded on this foundational work through numerous academic papers that have significantly contributed to my professional growth and scholarly advancements.

The original thesis, written in Arabic, served as a formal academic reference throughout my scholarly journey. However, given the profound significance of this topic in today's world—particularly within the field of comparative religious studies—I felt it imperative to make this research accessible to a wider audience. The importance of this subject is undeniable, especially as we navigate an era of increasing religious and cultural exchange.

When I began my doctoral research, discussions on interfaith dialogue, particularly the Abrahamic dialogue, were neither as widespread nor as prominent as they are today. At that time, resources on the topic were scarce, and scholarly attention was limited. Despite these challenges, the thesis emerged as a meaningful contribution to the field, addressing a critical intellectual gap and providing insights that resonate even more profoundly in our contemporary context.

Recognizing the need for broader accessibility, I have translated this work into English. This translation serves as a bridge for non-Arabic readers, extending the insights and discussions within this study to a global audience. Through this effort, I hope to foster a deeper understanding of the commonalities and differences among the Abrahamic religions and to encourage respectful dialogue and mutual learning among their adherents.

I express my sincere gratitude to Allah ﷻ for His guidance and strength throughout this journey. I dedicate this work to the pursuit of knowledge, peace, and mutual respect among all of humanity.

May Allah ﷻ accept this effort and grant it success.

The Author
Dr. Ali Mohamed Salah

# PART
# 1

# PATHS OF TRUTH AND SALVATION IN THE ABRAHAMIC RELIGIONS:

*Between "Pluralism and Exclusivism" - An Analytical Islamic Perspective*

## DR. ALI MOHAMED SALAH

## ABSTRACT

This research addresses the " **Paths of Truth and Salvation between Pluralism and Exclusivism in the Abrahamic Religions: An Islamic Analytical Perspective"** The aim is to analyze the positions of the Abrahamic religions (Judaism, Christianity, and Islam) regarding the concept of the path of truth and salvation in the contexts of pluralism and unity through a comparative and analytical study from an Islamic viewpoint.

The research focuses on providing an Islamic analytical perspective on the proposed idea, reviewing aspects that support or oppose this concept within Islamic thought. The study begins by highlighting the figure of the Prophet Abraham (peace be upon him) and his esteemed status within the Abrahamic religions. It also presents a comparative reading of the positions of each of the three religions regarding religious pluralism, emphasizing the sacred texts and intellectual interpretations formulated by these religions throughout history.

Furthermore, the research addresses important questions about the nature of the religion of Abraham (peace be upon him) and who truly belongs to it, offering an analytical description of the idea based on the Islamic perspective of doctrine and monotheism. The research clarifies how Islam views the status of other Abrahamic religions within the framework of absolute religious truth, while also examining the

possibility of coexistence among religions within a framework that acknowledges intellectual and existential pluralism, all while preserving the fundamental principles of each faith.

**Keywords:** **Abrahamic, Pluralism, Exclusivism, Affiliation, Truth, Salvation**

# ملخص البحث

يتناول هذا البحث موضوع «مسارات الحق والخلاص بين التعددية والإنحصارية في الأديان الإبراهيمية: رؤية إسلامية تحليلية"، حيث يهدف إلى تحليل موقف الأديان الإبراهيمية (اليهودية، المسيحية، والإسلام) تجاه مفهوم طريق الحق والخلاص في سياقات التعددية والوحدة من خلال دراسة مقارنة وتحليلية برؤية إسلامية. يركز البحث على تقديم رؤية تحليلية إسلامية للفكرة المطروحة ، مستعرضاً الجوانب التي تدعم أو تعارض هذا المفهوم في الفكر الإسلامي. تبدأ الدراسة بإبراز شخصية النبي إبراهيم (عليه السلام) ومكانته المرموقة في الديانات الإبراهيمية، كما تقدم الدراسة قراءة مقارنة لمواقف كل دين من الأديان الثلاثة تجاه التعددية الدينية، مع التركيز على النصوص المقدسة والتفسيرات الفكرية التي صاغتها هذه الأديان عبر العصور.

علاوة على ذلك، يعالج البحث تساؤلات مهمة حول طبيعة دين إبراهيم عليه السلام ومن ينتمي إليه حقاً، مع تقديم وصف تحليلي للفكرة بالاعتماد على الرؤية الإسلامية للعقيدة والتوحيد. يوضح البحث كيف ينظر الإسلام إلى مكانة الأديان الإبراهيمية الأخرى في إطار الحقيقة الدينية المطلقة، ويستعرض إمكانية تعايش الأديان ضمن إطار يعترف بالتعددية الفكرية والوجودية، مع الحفاظ على المبادئ الأساسية لكل دين.

الكلمات المفتاحية: إبراهيمية، تعددية، والإنحصارية ، إنتماء، الحق، الخلاص.

# FOUNDATIONAL OVERVIEW OF THE STUDY:
## OBJECTIVES, MOTIVATION, CHALLENGES, METHODOLOGY, AND FRAMEWORK

## RESEARCH OBJECTIVES

This study seeks to achieve the following objectives:

1. **Presenting the Authentic Methodology of Prophet Abraham's Religion:**
   To highlight the true and unaltered path of Prophet Abraham's religion, which adherents of the three Abrahamic faiths are called upon to follow.

2. **Unveiling the Authentic Life and Personality of Prophet Abraham:**
   To explore the true character and biography of Prophet Abraham as reflected in the Bible, juxtaposed against the Qur'anic portrayal—untainted by distortion and alteration, unlike previous scriptures.

3. **Highlighting Points of Agreement and Divergence:**
   To analyze areas of convergence and divergence among the three Abrahamic faiths concerning their discourse on truth, salvation, and deliverance.

4. **Engaging with the Perspectives of the Three Faiths:**
   To critically discuss the views of Judaism, Christianity, and Islam through the lens of Islamic teachings, drawing on evidence from the Qur'an, Hadith, and scholarly interpretations.

## REASONS FOR CHOOSING THE TOPIC

1. **Advancing Specialized Knowledge:**
   To enrich scholarly understanding by addressing a topic that merits deeper investigation.

2. **Simplifying Complex Concepts:**
   To present the subject matter in an accessible manner for non-specialist audiences, making critical knowledge more widely available.

3. **Responding to Community Suggestions:**
   This research was inspired by proposals from esteemed individuals, motivating the author to undertake this work with trust in Allah's support and guidance.

## PREVIOUS STUDIES:

- *The Contemporary Muslim Perspective on Other Religions* by Amir Al-Hafi

- *Towards a New Concept of Religious Pluralism* by Adnan Al-Maqrani

- *The Challenge of Religious Pluralism: A Christian Response* by John Hick

- *Religious Diversity and the American Experience: A Theological Introduction* by David Hollinger

- *Trialogue of the Abrahamic Faiths* by Ismail Raja

This research distinguishes itself by offering an Islamic analytical perspective on the various paths to truth and salvation, with a particular focus on how pluralism and exclusivism interact within the Abrahamic religions. It also seeks to analyze the cultural, historical, and political dimensions that shape these concepts, providing a comprehensive framework for understanding the differing positions within the three religions.

## RESEARCH PROBLEM

This study confronts several challenges, including:

- **Limited Sources:** A lack of comprehensive resources addressing the topic in-depth.

- **Conflicting Islamic Views:** Divergent opinions within Islamic discourse complicate the process of arriving at reliable conclusions.
- **Ambiguity in Interpretation:** Misinterpretations and contradictions by some authors create confusion about the topic.
- **Tensions Between Coexistence and Absolute Truth:** Navigating the balance between Islam's advocacy for peaceful coexistence and its adherence to absolute truth, which cannot be compromised.

## RESEARCH METHODOLOGY

The study adopts the **descriptive and analytical method**, foundational for research in philosophy, religion, humanities, and social sciences. This approach involves describing the phenomenon, analyzing similarities and differences, and synthesizing or weighing findings with evidence.

Additionally, the **analytical method** will be utilized, comprising three key processes:

1. **Interpretation (Deconstruction):** Breaking down complex ideas for deeper understanding.
2. **Critique (Evaluation):** Assessing and weighing concepts critically.
3. **Synthesis (Reconstruction):** Reassembling ideas into coherent frameworks.

These methods will facilitate a nuanced understanding of the subject, helping analyze the diverse dimensions of Abrahamic faiths.

## STRUCTURE OF THE RESEARCH

The research will be structured into:

1. Abstract and Introduction.
2. Two primary sections addressing the core arguments.
3. Conclusion, followed by recommendations.
4. Appendices and indexes.

## RESEARCH METHODOLOGY

The study adopts the **descriptive and analytical method**, foundational for research in philosophy, religion, humanities, and social sciences. This approach involves describing the phenomenon, analyzing similarities and differences, and synthesizing or weighing findings with evidence.

Additionally, the **analytical method** will be utilized, comprising three key processes:

1. **Interpretation (Deconstruction):** Breaking down complex ideas for deeper understanding.
2. **Critique (Evaluation):** Assessing and weighing concepts critically.
3. **Synthesis (Reconstruction):** Reassembling ideas into coherent frameworks.

These methods will facilitate a nuanced understanding of the subject, helping analyze the diverse dimensions of Abrahamic faiths.

## STRUCTURE OF THE RESEARCH

The research will be structured into:

1. Abstract and Introduction.
2. Two primary sections addressing the core arguments.
3. Conclusion, followed by recommendations.
4. Appendices and indexes.

## INTRODUCTION

Religious pluralism is among the most prominent contemporary issues sparking extensive debate among scholars and thinkers across various faiths, particularly the Abrahamic religions, which share profound monotheistic and historical roots.

This study, titled ***"Paths to Truth and Salvation Between Pluralism and Exclusivism in the Abrahamic Religions: An Analytical Islamic Perspective,"*** aims to explore the topic from two primary angles: first, by comparing the positions of the Abrahamic religions (Judaism, Christianity, and Islam) on the issue of religious pluralism, and second, by offering a critical analysis of the Islamic perspective on pluralism, examining both its aspects of acceptance and opposition, to clarify Islam's true stance on this critical matter.

While the concept of religious pluralism may appear relatively modern in some respects, its intellectual roots trace back to ancient discussions on the nature of truth in religions and the dynamics of engagement with the "other" who holds different beliefs.

The first part of this study introduces the figure of Prophet Abraham (peace be upon him) as portrayed in sacred texts and historical contexts, according to historians, archaeologists, and biographical records. It emphasizes his foundational role in establishing monotheism wherever he resided and his enduring influence on the followers of the Abrahamic faiths. The study also examines the stances of the three religions concerning the acceptance or rejection of religious pluralism, with a focus on the foundational texts of each religion and the interpretations of their scholars and thinkers. Additionally, it analyzes the historical contexts that shaped these positions over time.

The research also addresses pivotal questions, such as the true religion of Abraham (peace be upon him) and which among the adherents of the three faiths can genuinely claim to follow him. Although Islamic perspectives on religious pluralism are diverse and multifaceted, this study adopts an approach inspired by Islamic theology and monotheism, highlighting the role of the Islamic message in correcting prior religious misconceptions.

This section offers an analysis of both classical and contemporary Islamic views on religious pluralism and explores how Islam perceives the place of other Abrahamic religions within the framework of ultimate religious truth.

The study asserts that Islam does not oppose the possibility of coexistence among religions within a framework that acknowledges intellectual and existential pluralism, respects the distinctiveness of each faith, and upholds the fundamental principles that characterize each creed. This discussion becomes increasingly significant in light of the complexities of the modern world, where cultures and religions intersect in unprecedented ways, necessitating a deeper understanding of these relationships.

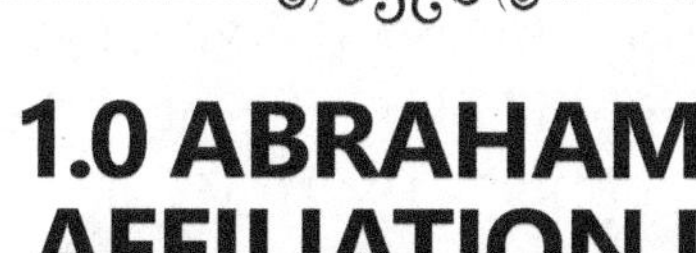

# 1.0 ABRAHAMIC AFFILIATION IN SACRED TEXTS

## 1.1 THE RELIGIOUS ESSENCE AND PERSONALITY OF ABRAHAM IN THE THREE SACRED SCRIPTURES

Abraham (peace be upon him) occupies a distinguished and venerated status in the sacred scriptures of Judaism, Christianity, and Islam—the Torah, the Gospel, and the Qur'an. Together, these Abrahamic faiths represent over a billion adherents worldwide. In Judaism, Abraham is honored as the patriarch of the Israelites and a spiritual forefather. The phrase "sitting in Abraham's bosom" symbolizes the ultimate reward in the afterlife for devout Jews, underscoring his pivotal role in their religious identity.

Christianity, too, reveres Abraham, drawing from Jewish traditions and honoring him as a model of faith. Islam, while recognizing this shared heritage, sees itself as a continuation of Abraham's monotheistic mission, emphasizing its direct lineage to his call for the worship of one God. This collective reverence has inspired generations of adherents from all three faiths to seek deeper, historically grounded insights into Abraham's life, character, and enduring spiritual legacy.

What cements Abraham's central role across these traditions is the convergence of their scriptures in portraying him as a paragon of devotion and faith. Each text exhorts its followers to emulate his example, presenting him as a unifying figure in humanity's shared spiritual journey.

The significance of Abraham as a unifying figure is further explored by the scholar Sidney Griffith, who references the influential Western academic Louis Massignon (1883–1962). Massignon's works extensively analyzed the Abrahamic connection, highlighting how Abraham serves as a symbol of shared heritage and common ground among Judaism, Christianity, and Islam. His insights affirm Abraham's enduring relevance as a bridge between these faiths, fostering dialogue and mutual understanding within the broader framework of their shared spiritual ancestry.

The writer states, quoting "Kuschel":

> For Christians this would mean that Abraham, as in the earliest New Testament writings, would be the figure of a person of faith. For Jews the Abraham of Genesis would become the norm for the Abraham of the Talmud and other rabbinical traditions. And for Muslims the Medinan narrowing of the significance of Abraham would recapture the original intentions of the prophetic revelation in Mecca, according to which the figure of Abraham was the model of faith in the one, only God to which Jews and Christians were invited to believe in him. [1]

Kuschel's analysis highlights the nuanced ways in which Abraham (peace be upon him) is understood within the three Abrahamic religions, each emphasizing aspects of his legacy that resonate with its theological framework. In Christianity, Abraham emerges as a figure of unwavering faith, as depicted in the earliest writings of the New Testament. His steadfast trust in God serves as a paradigm for Christian belief and devotion.

---

1  Islam and Christian Muslim Relations. Vol. 8, No. 2, July 1997, p. 207-208.

In Judaism, the Abraham of the Book of Genesis serves as the foundational archetype for later interpretations found in the Talmud and other rabbinical traditions. Here, Abraham's actions and covenantal relationship with God provide a normative framework for Jewish identity and practice.

Islam offers a perspective that both aligns with and reinterprets this legacy. The Medinan revelations, according to Kuschel, refine Abraham's significance to reaffirm the original intent of the Meccan prophetic message. Abraham is presented as the quintessential model of pure monotheistic faith, embodying submission to the one God. This portrayal simultaneously invites Jews and Christians to recognize and embrace this shared commitment to monotheism.

Through these distinct yet interconnected lenses, Kuschel illustrates how Abraham's legacy serves as both a unifying figure and a point of theological divergence among the three traditions, reflecting the richness and complexity of their shared heritage.

Abraham's (peace be upon him) life story has captivated historians, archaeologists, and biographers, both Muslim and non-Muslim, who have dedicated extensive efforts to uncover the historical truths surrounding this pivotal figure. Among these endeavors, archaeology stands out for its focused attempts to trace the life of the "Father of the Prophets." Few historical figures have drawn such intense archaeological interest, with expeditions to Iraq, Palestine, and Egypt seeking to unearth the hidden relics and mysteries that hold the keys to understanding the profound legacy of Abraham and his influence on the human spirit and conscience.[2]

Archaeological findings suggest that Abraham lived around the 19th century BCE, approximately four thousand years ago. Al-Mas'udi, the renowned Muslim historian, calculated that 567 years separated

---

2  Abbas Mahmud al-Aqqad. Ibrahim, Abu al-Anbiya'. (n.d.). Maktabat al-'Asriyya, Beirut. p. 3.

Abraham's time from the Exodus of Moses, offering a framework for understanding his historical placement.[3]

While most historians agree that Abraham was born in Iraq, opinions diverge regarding the exact location. Some identify his birthplace as "Ur" of the Chaldeans, others suggest "Uruk" or "Kutha," and some associate it with "Birs Nimrud," believed to be the site of the attempted burning of Abraham. Among these, the majority of Islamic sources point to "Kutha" as his birthplace, an ancient center of the Semitic peoples in Iraq. These peoples, including Abraham's ancestors, had migrated from the Arabian Peninsula to settle along the banks of the Euphrates River.

Abraham is traditionally linked to the Aramean tribes, Semitic groups originating from the Arabian Peninsula. His family's migration to Iraq reflects broader movements of Arab tribes seeking new settlements along the Euphrates. This historical context situates Abraham within a dynamic landscape of cultural and tribal interactions, underscoring his enduring significance across religious and historical narratives. Professor Daidies states:

> 66 The family of Abraham (peace be upon him) had come to the land of Babylon from the land of Canaan, which was their original homeland.[4] 99

## 1.2 HIS MISSIONARY EFFORTS AND ENDURING STRUGGLE

Abraham (peace be upon him) exemplified unwavering dedication in his mission to spread the message of monotheism. His efforts transcended geographical boundaries and traditional methods, as he journeyed across Babylon, Egypt, and Harran. Guided by the divine intellect and wisdom bestowed upon him, he employed reasoned arguments and profound insight to instill belief in the oneness of God among his people. His

---

3  Susah, Ahmad Susah. Mufassal al-'Arab wa al-Yahud fi al-Tarikh. 1392 AH/1972 CE. Manshurat Wizarat al-I'lam, Baghdad, Iraq. First edition. pp. 506-520

4  Daidies, S. (1910). The Jews in Babylonia. London: London Press. p. 7.

mission aimed to liberate them from the false worship of idols and celestial bodies, redirecting their devotion to the Creator of the heavens and the earth.

Abraham's approach was marked by persistence, adaptability, and compassion. His comprehensive call to faith addressed not only the practices of idol worship but also the philosophical inclinations of his audience, such as their reverence for celestial phenomena. Through reasoned discourse and an exemplary personal character, he inspired reflection and transformation, striving to guide humanity toward the worship of the one true God.

This relentless struggle and universal call earned Abraham a singular honor in the Qur'an: a unique and unparalleled title. The Qur'an describes him as a *ḥanīf* (pure monotheist) and as an *ummah* (a leader or model for all humanity), a recognition granted to no other prophet before or after him. This distinction underscores his exceptional role in the history of divine guidance, solidifying his legacy as the father of monotheism and a beacon for all who seek to follow the straight path.

As Allah ﷻ says:

> **66** *Abraham was indeed a model, Devoutly obedient to God, (And) true in faith, and he Joined not gods with God :* **He showed his gratitude For the favours of God, Who chose him, and guided him To a Straight Way. And We gave him Good In this world, and he will be, In the Hereafter, in the ranks Of the Righteous.**
>
> (Sūra 16: Nahl, verses:120-123). **99**

Furthermore, Allah ﷻ described him as His close friend, saying:

> **66** *For God did take Abraham for a friend."*
>
> (Sūra 4: Nisāa, verse: 125). **99**

Additionally, Allah, ﷻ attributed the faith to him, calling it his *millah* (way), saying:

> **"And who turns away from the religion of Abraham but such as debase their souls with folly? Him We chose and rendered pure in this world: and he will be in the Hereafter in the ranks of the righteous'"** Behold! his Lord said to him: **"Bow (thy will to me)"** He said: **"I bow (my will) to the Lord and Cherisher of the universe."** And this was the legacy that Abraham left to his sons and so did Jacob; **"O my sons! God hath chosen the faith for you; then die not except in the faith of Islam"**.
>
> (Sūra 2: Baqara, verses: 130-132).

## 1.3 THE MESSAGE OF ABRAHAM (PEACE BE UPON HIM):

The message of Abraham (peace be upon him) to his people can be summarized in three main forms of idolatry that his people were immersed in:

- The first: The worship of idols, which they inherited from the people of Noah, 'Ad, and Thamud.

- The second: The worship of celestial bodies, including the sun, moon, and stars, which was one of their innovations.

- The third: The worship of kings who claimed divinity, the first of whom was Nimrod, the son of Canaan.

Allah ﷻ sent Abraham (peace be upon him) to fight against these three types of corruption, disbelief, and misguidance[5].

## 1.4 ABRAHAM (PEACE BE UPON HIM) AND HIS NARRATIVE IN THE OLD TESTAMENT

The Old Testament, particularly the Book of Genesis, offers one of the most detailed accounts of Abraham's life, positioning him as a

---

5 Adam Abdullah al-Aluri. Tārīkh al-Da'wah Bayn al-Ams wa al-Yawm. 1408 AH/1988 CE. Matba'at Dar al-Tadamun, Cairo. p. 59.

central figure in biblical history. Genesis traces Abraham's lineage back to Shem, the son of Noah, establishing a genealogical connection of immense theological significance. According to this account, Abraham is identified as the son of Nahor, son of Serug, son of Reu, son of Peleg, son of Eber, son of Arphaxad, son of Shem, son of Noah.[6] This lineage situates Abraham within a divine covenantal history, linking him to Noah's legacy and highlighting his role as a chosen figure in the unfolding divine plan.

The narrative further focuses on the family of Terah, Abraham's father, who had three sons: Abram (later renamed Abraham), Nahor, and Haran. Haran, the father of Lot, died during Terah's lifetime in "Ur of the Chaldeans," the family's homeland. This specific identification of Abraham's origins in "Ur of the Chaldeans" reinforces his connection to Mesopotamian civilization and its rich cultural and historical context.

By presenting Abraham as emerging from a distinguished ancestral line, Genesis emphasizes his foundational role in biblical history. This genealogical tradition not only underscores Abraham's significance as a patriarch of faith but also positions him as a key figure through whom God's promises and covenantal blessings would be realized, shaping the religious identity of subsequent generations in Judaism, Christianity, and beyond.

The following outlines the detailed account of Abraham's life as presented in the Book of Genesis within the Old Testament:

> 66 These are the generations of Terah: Terah fathered Abram, Nahor, and Haran; and Haran fathered Lot. Haran died in the presence of his father Terah in the land of his birth, in Ur of the Chaldeans. And Abram and Nahor took wives. The name of Abram's wife was Sarai, and the name of Nahor's wife was Milcah, the daughter of Haran, the father of Milcah and Iscah. Now Sarai was barren; she had no child.

---

6 Serug, son of Reu, son of Peleg, son of Eber, son of Shelah, son of Arphaxad, son of Shem, son of Noah (peace be upon him). See, Abd al-Salam Harun. *Tahdhib Sirat Ibn Hisham.* 8th ed., Beirut, Lebanon, 1401 AH - 1981, p. 17.

Terah took Abram his son, and Lot the son of Haran, his grandson, and Sarai his daughter-in-law, his son Abram's wife, and they went forth together from Ur of the Chaldeans to go into the land of Canaan. But when they came to Haran, they settled there. The days of Terah were 205 years, and Terah died in Haran".[7]

This genealogical chain underscores the unbroken lineage from Noah to Serug, culminating in the pivotal figure of Abraham (peace be upon him), a connection affirmed in both biblical and Islamic traditions. Abraham's life, as recounted in the Torah, reflects a narrative of relentless journeys, enduring struggles, steadfast perseverance, and unwavering dedication to righteousness and the dissemination of God's message.

Abraham's mission brought him peace of heart as he witnessed the solid establishment of God's faith on earth. His sons, Ishmael and Isaac, carried forward his legacy in their respective regions. Ishmael, appointed as a prophet and messenger, oversaw the spiritual and communal affairs of the Muslims in the Arabian Peninsula, centered in Mecca. Meanwhile, Isaac, also a prophet, worked to spread God's religion among the Canaanites, continuing Abraham's efforts to guide humanity toward monotheism.

As Abraham approached the fulfillment of his mission, he settled in Hebron, devoting his remaining years to worship and preparing for his meeting with his Creator. His life concluded in a state of spiritual fulfillment and divine proximity, his soul ascending to its Lord at the age of 175. Abraham's extraordinary journey, marked by faith, devotion, and the propagation of monotheism, solidifies his status as a patriarch and a guiding light for generations across Judaism, Christianity, and Islam.

---

7  In Genesis, Chapter 11:27–32 (ESV Translation)

## 1.5 ABRAHAM (PEACE BE UPON HIM) AND HIS NARRATIVE IN THE NEW TESTAMENT

The scholar Abbas Mahmoud al-Aqqad observes that the New Testament, encompassing the four Gospels alongside the teachings of the apostles and disciples, does not significantly expand upon the narrative of Abraham (peace be upon him) as it is detailed in the Book of Genesis and other Old Testament texts. However, al-Aqqad argues that the New Testament introduces a transformative perspective on Abraham's role, reflecting the theological developments and challenges faced by the Jewish community during the time of Jesus' birth[8].

This shift is particularly apparent in three pivotal religious themes:

1. **The Concept of Life After Death:** The New Testament engages with the evolving Jewish understanding of the afterlife, a concept that gained prominence during the intertestamental period. Abraham is invoked in discussions of eternal life and resurrection, symbolizing the righteous who are rewarded in the afterlife. Phrases such as "Abraham's bosom" in Luke's Gospel (16:22-23) serve as metaphors for the comfort and salvation awaiting the faithful, positioning Abraham as a guardian figure in the eschatological narrative.

2. **The Divine Promise:** Abraham's covenant with God, central to the Old Testament, is reinterpreted in the New Testament to emphasize its spiritual dimensions. The apostle Paul, in particular, highlights Abraham as the father of faith, whose righteousness stems from belief rather than adherence to the law (Romans 4:13-16). This redefinition broadens the scope of the divine promise, extending it to all who share Abraham's faith, regardless of their ethnic or cultural lineage.

3. **The Spiritual and Physical Realms:** The New Testament shifts the focus from the physical inheritance of the land promised to Abraham to a spiritual inheritance encompassing all believers. This universalization underscores the inclusivity of Abraham's legacy as

---

8  Ibrahim, Abu al-Anbiya. (p. 44).

a model of faith, bridging the divide between Jewish and Gentile followers of Christ.

Through these theological developments, the New Testament portrays Abraham not only as a historical and ancestral figure but also as a timeless exemplar of faith, whose legacy transcends cultural and temporal boundaries to serve as a cornerstone of Christian doctrine.

## 1.6 ABRAHAM (PEACE BE UPON HIM) AND HIS FAITH IN QUR'ANIC STUDIES

The Qur'an, as the final divine revelation, affirms the existence of Abraham (peace be upon him) and highlights his mission as one rooted in pure monotheism, entirely free from polytheism and doubt. This portrayal aligns with the core themes found in the sacred texts of Judaism and Christianity but distinguishes itself through the depth and clarity of its narrative.

A comparative analysis of the Torah, the Gospel, and the Qur'an reveals that the Qur'an offers a more comprehensive account of Abraham's life and mission. Unlike the earlier scriptures, the Qur'anic narration employs a unique and varied style, presenting Abraham's story in a logical sequence that resonates with human understanding and appeals to the intellect. This approach ensures that the narrative remains accessible and impactful, even for those hesitant to rely solely on historical accounts.

Historical reports, when subjected to rigorous scientific scrutiny, often reveal inconsistencies or limitations. In contrast, the Qur'an provides a narrative that transcends such flaws, presenting spiritual truths with coherence and depth. The Qur'anic depiction of Abraham emphasizes his unwavering faith, his rejection of idolatry, and his steadfast commitment to spreading the belief in one God.

Through its approach, the Qur'an not only reinforces Abraham's status as a model of faith but also elevates his story to a universal message, offering guidance that transcends the constraints of time and historical documentation. Abraham's narrative in the Qur'an thus serves as a profound testament to the enduring power of monotheism and its ability to inspire across generations.

Allah ﷻ says:

"And remember that Abraham was tried by his Lord with certain commands which he fulfilled; He said: "I will make thee an Imam to the nations." He pleaded: "And also (Imams) from my offspring!" He answered: "But my promise is not within the reach of evil-doers."

"Remember We made the house a place of assembly for men and a place of safety; and take ye the station of Abraham as a place of prayer; and We covenanted with Abraham and Isma'il that they should sanctify My House for those who compass it round or use it as a retreat or bow or prostrate themselves (therein in prayer).

"And remember Abraham said: "My Lord make this a City of Peace and feed its people with fruits such of them as believe in God and the Last Day." He said: "(Yea) and such as reject faith for a while will I grant them their pleasure but will soon drive them to the torment of fire an evil destination (indeed)!"

"And remember Abraham and Isma'il raised the foundations of the House (with this prayer): "Our Lord! accept (this service) from us for thou art the All-Hearing the All-Knowing.

"Our Lord! make of us Muslims bowing to Thy (Will) and of our progeny a people Muslim bowing to Thy (Will) and show us our places for the celebration of (due) rites; and turn unto us (in mercy); for Thou art the Oft-Returning Most-Merciful.

"Our Lord! send amongst them an Apostle of their own who shall rehearse Thy Signs to them and instruct them in Scripture and Wisdom and sanctify them; for Thou art the Exalted in Might the Wise."

"And who turns away from the religion of Abraham but such as debase their souls with folly? Him We chose and rendered pure in this world: and he will be in the Hereafter in the ranks of the righteous."

"Behold! his Lord said to him: "Bow (thy will to me)" He said: "I bow (my will) to the Lord and Cherisher of the universe.""

**"And this was the legacy that Abraham left to his sons and so did Jacob; "O my sons! God hath chosen the faith for you; then die not except in the faith of Islam."** Sūra 2: Baqara, verses: 124-132

These are a series of verses in the Qur'an that elaborate on the life of Abraham (peace be upon him) or allude to his mission, which contains elements that prefigure the Islamic call.

The Qur'an provides a comprehensive portrayal of Abraham's life, his devotion to God, and his pioneering role in the message of monotheism, which lays the foundation for the later advent of Islam. The verses highlight both his personal journey and the broader significance of his mission in shaping the path of faith, demonstrating the continuity of divine guidance leading to the final revelation.

Dr. Salah al-Khalidi states:

> 66 The main sects and groups that have disputed their connection to Abraham (peace be upon him) are four: the Jews, the Christians, the polytheistic Arabs, and the Muslims. The Jews claimed to be descendants of Abraham and asserted that they followed his faith—even though, in practice, they did not. They treated religion as an inheritance, passing it down as they would material wealth, regardless of whether they adhered to it or structured their lives around his guidance. Since when has religion and guidance been a 'commodity' passed from parents to children, inherited like material possessions?"[9] 99

The Qur'anic portrayal of Abraham (peace be upon him) provides a definitive account of the faith he practiced, leaving no room for ambiguity or contention among those who claim adherence to his religion. The Qur'an underscores Abraham's role as a paradigm of guidance, obedience, gratitude, and devotion to God, presenting him as an enduring example of faith for humanity.

---

9  Dr. Salah al-Khalidi. Haqa'iq Qur'aniyya Hawl al-Qadiyya al-Filastiniyya. 1994, Manshurat Filastin al-Muslima, London, pp. 58-59.

One of the most profound descriptions of Abraham in the Qur'an is as an *ummah*—a term rich in meaning, often interpreted as representing an entire community. This characterization reflects Abraham's embodiment of collective virtues: goodness, obedience, and divine blessings. Furthermore, the Qur'an identifies him as an *imam*, a leader whose exemplary conduct and unwavering commitment to monotheism serve as a blueprint for others. Through his faith and actions, Abraham not only secured his own reward but also the reward of those who emulate his guidance, amplifying his impact across generations.

This portrayal elevates Abraham from being a solitary individual to a symbol of collective righteousness. His life encapsulates the virtues of a leader and a role model, making him a central figure in the spiritual imagination of all who follow the path of monotheism.[10] By presenting Abraham in this way, the Qur'an solidifies his status not only as a pivotal historical figure but also as an eternal beacon of piety and faith. His legacy continues to inspire and guide, demonstrating the enduring relevance of his mission in the lives of believers across time.

In articulating the connection between the religion of Abraham peace be upon him and that of Muhammad ﷺ, Allah ﷻ says:

> ❝ **Say: Verily my Lord hath guided me to a way that is straight a religion of right the path (trod) by Abraham the true in faith and he (certainly) joined not gods with God.**"
>
> Sūra 6: An'āmm verse:161) ❞

The verse from Sūra 6: An'āmm, verse 161—"Say: Verily my Lord hath guided me to a way that is straight, a religion of right, the path trodden by Abraham the true in faith, and he certainly joined not gods with God"—illuminates the profound connection between the faith of

---

10  Qutb, Sayyid. Fi Zilal al-Qur'an. 13th ed., 1987, Dar al-Shorouk, Cairo, vol. 4, p. 2200.

Abraham (peace be upon him) and that of Muhammad ﷺ, the Seal of the Messengers.

In this verse, Allah ﷻ commands His Prophet ﷺ to declare the divine favor granted to him: guidance to the straight path—a path of unwavering truth and righteousness. This path, which leads to success both in this world and the hereafter, is the same pure monotheism that Abraham followed, and that all believers are called to adhere to. Abraham (peace be upon him), as a figure of unshakable faith, stands as the model for this straight and steadfast path.

The religion referred to in the verse is the ultimate truth—pure devotion to Allah ﷻ alone. It is the faith that all the prophets and messengers, from Adam to Muhammad ﷺ, conveyed to their communities. This religion sharply contrasts with the practices of the polytheists of Arabia, particularly the leaders of the Quraysh, who claimed to follow the way of Abraham but deviated from its essence by incorporating idolatry. Similarly, it also diverges from the interpretations of the People of the Book (Jews and Christians), who, while claiming alignment with the legacy of Abraham, Moses, and Jesus (peace be upon them all), have altered the foundational teachings of monotheism in their respective traditions.[11]

This verse thus emphasizes that the true faith, as represented by Abraham (peace be upon him) and conveyed through Muhammad ﷺ, is a path of pure, uncompromising monotheism, rejecting any form of polytheism or deviation from the straight path. It is a reminder that the faith of the prophets is one and the same, a call to worship Allah alone, which continues to resonate through the Qur'anic message.

In short, Islam is the intersection of the message of all the prophets—a universal truth acceptable to Allah. As Allah ﷻ declares:

**"The Religion before God is Islam (submission to His will):."** *(Sūra 3: Āl-i-ʿImrān, verse: 19)*

------

11  Al-Tafsir Al-Munir (8/124).

In addressing the relationship between Abraham's faith, Islam, and other religions, Allah ﷻ further states:

> Ye people of the Book! why dispute ye about Abraham when the Law and the Gospel were not revealed till after him? Have ye no under- standing?"
>
> "Ah! ye are those who fell to disputing (even) in matters of which ye had some knowledge! but why dispute ye in matters of which ye have no knowledge? It is God Who knows and ye who know not!"
>
> "Abraham was not a Jew nor yet a Christian but he was true in faith and bowed his will to God's (which is Islam) and he joined not gods with God".
>
> "Without doubt among men the nearest of kin to Abraham are those who follow him as are also this Apostle and those who believe; and God is the Protector of those who have faith".
>
> (Sūra 3: Āl-i-'Imrān, verses: 65-68)

Through the Qur'anic verses, Allah ﷻ makes it abundantly clear that Abraham (peace be upon him) was neither a Jew nor a Christian, as both of these traditions emerged long after his time. Rather, he was a monotheist—a Muslim in the purest sense—devoted entirely to the worship of Allah ﷻ and free from any association with polytheism. This declaration places Abraham firmly within the realm of true submission to God, and it is his way of monotheistic faith that serves as the rightful heritage for all who follow the path of sincere belief.

The true heirs to Abraham's legacy are those who align themselves with his example, including the Prophet Muhammad ﷺ and his followers, as well as anyone who sincerely submits to Allah ﷻ. This spiritual lineage connects the followers of Islam directly to the heart of Abraham's faith, binding them in a religion that emphasizes sincerity, submission, and complete alignment with divine will.

The Qur'an, in rejecting the claims of both Jewish and Christian communities to exclusive affiliation with Abraham, dismantles any notion that he was a part of their respective traditions. The assertion that Abraham was a Jew or a Christian is baseless, for both Judaism and Christianity came into existence long after his time, and their scriptures—the Torah and the Gospel—were revealed long after he had lived. As such, the claim to be a "descendant" of Abraham through religion is theologically unfounded.

The Qur'an thus rejects the notion that Abraham could be considered a part of either the Jewish or Christian traditions. His faith, founded on pure monotheism, is independent of the later developments of both religions. The connection that truly matters in matters of faith is not genealogical or based on physical descent, but spiritual inheritance—adhering to the beliefs of one's predecessors and emulating their commitment to submission to God.

While both Jews and Christians may trace their lineage to Abraham through physical descent, their claims of spiritual inheritance are questionable. This is because they do not fully uphold the core tenets of Abraham's faith. As the Prophet Muhammad ﷺ aptly stated:

> 66 **But he who is made slow by his actions will not be speeded by his genealogy**".[12] 99

This powerful statement emphasizes that it is not one's bloodline that grants closeness to God, but one's faith and actions. True spiritual connection to Abraham is measured by the degree to which one adheres to his pure, monotheistic submission to Allah ﷻ.

This principle is vividly illustrated in the story of the Prophet Noah and his son, as recounted in the Qur'an. Despite their biological relationship, Noah's son was disowned spiritually due to his lack of righteous action:

---

12  Mishkat al-Masabih 204, Book 2, Hadith 7, https://sunnah.com/mishkat:204

> *And Noah called upon His Lord, and said : "O my Lord ! surely My son is of my family ! And Thy promise is true, And Thou art The Justest of Judges !*
> He said : " O Noah ! He is not of thy family : For his conduct is unrighteous. So ask not of Me That of which thou Hast no knowledge ! I give thee counsel, lest Thou act like the ignorant ! "
>
> *(Surah Hud: 45–46).*

Regarding Abraham, the Qur'an affirms:

> *Abraham was indeed a model, Devoutly obedient to God, (And) true in faith, and he Joined not gods with God :*
> He showed his gratitude For the favours of God, Who chose him, and guided him To a Straight Way.
>
> (Sūra 16: Nahl, verses: 120–121)

## 1.7 THE TRUTH OF ABRAHAM'S FAITH AND HIS TRUE FOLLOWERS

The Qur'anic verses unequivocally establish the truth of Abraham's (peace be upon him) faith. He was a follower of Islam—the upright religion of submission to Allah. His path was one of pure monotheism, and his true followers are those who align themselves with this faith. Allah is the ally and protector of all believers who adhere to this righteous path.

In conclusion, any claim to belong to Abraham's legacy that does not involve following his example of submission to Allah is nothing more than an empty assertion. These claims, driven by disputation rather than genuine faith, do not alter the reality of his legacy. They fail to establish a true and meaningful connection to Abraham's life and teachings. True affiliation with Abraham comes not through mere descent or verbal assertions, but through faithfully following his example of unwavering devotion to Allah and his commitment to the oneness of God. The essence of his legacy is the path of pure monotheism and submission, which continues to be the foundation of Islam.

## 1.8 UNIQUE INSIGHTS OF THE QUR'AN REGARDING ABRAHAM (PEACE BE UPON HIM):

The Qur'an provides distinct accounts about Abraham (peace be upon him) that stand apart from those found in other scriptures, such as the Torah and the Gospels. These unique aspects can be categorized into two main themes:

1.  **Historical Events**:
    The Qur'an uniquely highlights specific incidents, such as Abraham and Ishmael raising the foundations of the Kaaba near the Sacred House in Mecca. This narrative is absent in earlier scriptures and emphasizes the connection between Abraham and the central Islamic sanctuary.

2.  **Religious Perspective**:
    The Qur'an presents a profound and clear distinction between idolatry and pure monotheism across the span of time between the composition of the Old Testament and the emergence of Islam. This perspective underscores the Qur'an's emphasis on the transcendence of Allah ﷻ and the rejection of anthropomorphism in worship, setting it apart from earlier religious texts.

Through these contributions, the Qur'an offers a definitive and comprehensive account of Abraham's life, mission, and faith, surpassing other sources that address his story. Interestingly, pre-Islamic Arab sources make no mention of Abraham or his monotheistic legacy. However, this omission does not imply that pre-Islamic Arabs were entirely unaware of Abraham. As some Western scholars have noted:

> 66 'We turn now to a consideration of Abraham as reflected in the Koran and the later Muslim religious literature. The first thing to be stated in this connection is prior to the

Koranic references to Abraham, whose name appears in it in the Arabicized form of Abraham, there is no mention of Abraham in any Arabic literary source or archaeological find. True, pre-Koranic Arabic sources show very sparely, so that the absence of any reference in them to Abraham cannot be taken as a proof that Abraham was unknown to the Arabs in the Jahiliya."[13]

The Qur'anic verses reaffirm the religious truths established by Abraham without alteration, aside from the necessary contextual adjustments for changing circumstances and societal developments. These adjustments resulted in specific laws and rulings that aligned with the needs of the time.

Ultimately, the Qur'an presents Abraham's message as a universal call for all people to remember and embrace the monotheism and spiritual heritage they have inherited from their forefather. His legacy is upheld as a timeless model of devotion, purity, and unwavering faith in Allah ﷻ. The Western scholar Massignon states:

The goal of the Qur'anic revelation is not to disclose and to justify any supernatural data unknown up to its time, but to make minds rediscover, and to recall to them the name of God, the temporal and eternal sanctions, the natural religion, the primordial law, the very simple cult which God had prescribed forever, which Adam, Abraham and the prophets practiced under the same forms."[14]

---

13  Raphael Patai, The Seed of Abraham. Jews and Arabs in Contact and Conflict, University of Utah Press, Salt Lake City, Utah, 1986, p.18.
14  Islam and Christian, Muslim Relations, Vol. no. 2, July 1997, p. 202.

## 1.9 DEFINING THE CONCEPT OF ABRAHAMIC AFFILIATION IN LIGHT OF QUR'ANIC TEXTS:

One of the verses that articulates this concept is Allah's statement:

> **The same religion has He Established for you as that Which He enjoined on Noah—The which We have sent By inspiration to thee—And that which We enjoined On Abraham, Moses, and Jesus : Namely, that ye should remain Steadfast in Religion, and make No divisions therein : To those who worship Other things than God, Hard is the (way) To which thou callest them. God chooses to Himself Those whom He pleases, And guides to Himself Those who turn (to Him)."**
>
> **"And they became divided Only after knowledge Reached them,—through selfish Envy as between themselves. Had it not been For a Word that Went forth before From thy Lord, (Tending) to a Term appointed, The matter would have Been settled between them : But truly those who have Inherited the Book after them Are in suspicious (disquieting) Doubt concerning it".**
>
> **"Now then, for that (reason), Call (them to the Faith), And stand steadfast As thou art commanded, Nor follow thou their vain Desires ; but say : " I believe In the Book which God has sent down ; And I am commanded To judge justly between you. God is Our Lord And your Lord. For us (Is the responsibility for) Our deeds, and for you For your deeds. There is No contention between us And you. God will Bring us together, And to Him is (Our) final goal".**
>
> Sūra 42: Shūra, verses:13–15).

The Qur'anic message asserts that the religion ordained for the followers of Muhammad is the same as that prescribed for Noah, Abraham, Moses, and Jesus. It raises pressing questions: Why, then, do the followers of Moses and Jesus diverge? Why do various Christian denominations contend with one another? Why do the followers of Moses and Jesus stand in opposition to the followers of Muhammad? Why do those who claim adherence to Abraham's faith, yet embrace idolatry, clash with Muslims? Why not unite under the banner carried by the final messenger, Muhammad, whose mission aligns with the unified directive: **"that ye should remain Steadfast in Religion, and make No divisions therein."**

This religion calls for unity under a singular banner, a banner raised successively by Noah, Abraham, Moses, and Jesus—peace be upon them all—culminating with Muhammad, peace and blessings be upon him, in the final covenant.[15]

## 1.10 INSIGHTS DERIVED FROM THE VERSES:

The aforementioned verses highlight several key truths:

1. **Unity of Divine Messages**: All revealed religions share the same fundamental principles, despite differences in secondary laws and practices.

2. **Continuity of Divine Law**: Islam builds upon the same divine guidance given to Noah, Abraham, Moses, and Jesus, emphasizing monotheism, obedience to God, belief in His messengers and scriptures, the afterlife, and core moral principles.

3. **Rejection of Polytheism**: The essence of true religion is the worship of one God, fundamentally incompatible with idolatry. This is why the concept of monotheism, epitomized by *La ilaha illa Allah* (There is no deity but God), challenges the polytheistic mindset.

4. **Skepticism Among Inheritors of Scripture**: Those who inherited the Torah and Gospel remain in doubt and confusion about their scriptures and the prophets' teachings.

---

15  Fi Zilal al-Qur'an* (5/3148).

## 1.11 SCRIPTURAL PERSPECTIVES ON ABRAHAMIC AFFILIATION: RAPHAEL PATAI'S VIEW

Raphael Patai summarizes Abraham's faith into three principal elements:

1. **Theological Element**: Belief in the one God.
2. **Moral Element**: Uprightness and justice.
3. **Ritual Element**: Circumcision.[16]

These elements converge in Islam, which invites all to embrace it as the true faith revealed by God. Islam is not only the culmination of previous divine messages but also a unique and independent system of truth, with laws suited to the time and circumstances of its revelation.

---

16  The Seed of Abraham, p. 17

# 2.0 RELIGIOUS PLURALISM WITHIN THE FRAMEWORK OF ABRAHAMIC AFFILIATION:

## PERSPECTIVES AND POSITIONS

## 2.1 THE DEFINING CHARACTERISTIC OF ABRAHAMIC AFFILIATION:

True religion, in its essence and entirety, is fundamentally a call for unity, harmony, and mutual affection. This principle is not confined to its spiritual ethos and core values alone but is deeply embedded in the explicit texts of divine revelation, both in their apparent meanings and deeper implications. It is not a concept derived through inference or speculation, but rather, it is the very foundation and ultimate purpose of religion. This intrinsic truth shapes the form and content of religion and acts as the benchmark by which all religious messages and practices are evaluated throughout the history of divine revelation.

At its core, true religion is singular in nature because its source, essence, and ultimate goal are unified. This unity has persisted across all stages of human history. From Adam and Noah to Abraham, Moses, Jesus, and finally Muhammad, peace and blessings be upon them all, each prophet has been part of a single, uninterrupted procession. They each delivered God's messages, which together reveal the essence of true religion to humanity across different times and places.

In this context, the Qur'an preserves a comprehensive understanding of the prophetic tradition by employing the term *Islam* universally. This term, which denotes submission, worship, and devotion to God alone in both thought and action, encompasses the core belief of monotheism (*tawhid*). This belief in the oneness of God has been the hallmark of every prophetic message, making it both the essence and primary characteristic of true religion.

With this understanding of Islam as the doctrine of monotheism and the unified mission of the prophets, one can appreciate the divine command revealed to the final prophet, Muhammad ﷺ, as a continuation of this timeless message. The message remains steadfast, calling all to the same truth: the pure worship and submission to Allah ﷻ alone. Allah ﷻ says to His prophet Muhammad ﷺ:

> 66 **Say: "Nay! but I am commanded to be the first of those who bow to God (in Islam) and be not thou of the company of those who join gods with God."'**
>
> *(Sūra 6: An'ām, Verse: 14)* 99

This foundational principle resolves all disputes and guides all dialogues. It serves as the standard against which claims are assessed and movements are measured:

> 66 **So if they dispute with thee say: "I have submitted my whole self to God and so have those who follow me." And say to the people of the Book and to those who are unlearned: "Do ye (also) submit yourselves?" If they do they are in right guidance but if they turn back thy duty is to convey the Message; and in God's sight are (all) His servants. (Sūra 3: Āl-i-'Imrān, verse: 20)** 99

Thus, the criterion of true religion—acknowledging God's oneness and submitting to Him alone—leaves no room for hesitation or ambiguity between disbelief and faith. It is an enduring standard, a precise scale that applies to all, including those who claim to follow fragments of previous revelations. As long as it is acknowledged that monotheism and submission to God are the essence of all divine messages, this principle remains the essence of true religion.

## 2.2 THE CONCEPT OF RELIGIOUS PLURALISM:

The concept of religious pluralism, rooted in the philosophy of religion, emerges from the reality of a world where multiple religions and ideologies coexist. In such a context, it suggests that mutual understanding and peaceful coexistence are not only possible but desirable. This coexistence is cultivated through the recognition and acceptance of diverse beliefs and practices. While the concept does not have a singular, universally accepted foundational principle, it has nonetheless become an influential force, shaping discussions and advancements across philosophy, religion, society, and politics.[17]

Religious pluralism exists alongside two other significant perspectives: religious exclusivism and religious inclusivism.

A deeper exploration of these two competing perspectives—exclusivism and inclusivism—offers valuable insight into the broader concept of pluralism itself.

## 2.3 RELIGIOUS EXCLUSIVISM:

Religious exclusivism is the belief that only one religion holds the exclusive path to salvation, happiness, and ultimate success. Adherents of this perspective argue that the true and complete understanding

---

17  Majallat Al-Tawhid (1997). Issue (87), Fifteenth Year, Dhu al-Qaʻdah 1417 AH - March, article published in the journal titled: "Al-Taʻaddudiyyah Al-Diniyyah: Nazrah Tahliliyyah" by Muhammad Ridha Al-Hijazi, translated by Alaa Al-Ridha'i (p. 47).

of reality and the divine is contained solely within their religion, and that following this path is the only way to achieve genuine fulfillment. According to religious exclusivism, all other religions fall short of revealing the ultimate truth and therefore cannot lead their followers to salvation.

This viewpoint is commonly held across a wide range of religious traditions. Nearly every major religion contains some form of exclusivist belief, asserting that its own teachings are the only valid means of attaining spiritual success. For adherents, this often means that belief and adherence to the specific doctrines and practices of their faith is indispensable for salvation, while the teachings of other religions are seen as insufficient or misguided.

This perspective is evident in the beliefs of the followers of the three major monotheistic religions:

- **Judaism** holds that the Israelites are God's chosen people and that Judaism is the sole path to happiness and success.

- **Christianity** proclaims, as stated in the Bible, that:

> 66 **Jesus answered, 'I am the way and the truth and the life. No one comes to the Father except through me.**"[18]   99

Additionally, the historical Christian doctrine emphasized:

> 66 **Outside the church, there is no salvation."**
> "He cannot have God as his Father who does not have the Church as his mother."[19]   99

- **Islam** similarly provides numerous evidences and texts affirming this exclusive view. For instance, the Qur'an declares:

---

18  John 14:6, NIV
19  *De Unitate Ecclesiae*, Chapter 6.

> **The Religion before God is Islam (submission to His will)."**
>
> *(Sūra 3: Āl-i-ʿImrān, verse: 19)* 

And:

> **If anyone desires a religion other than Islam (submission to God) never will it be accepted of him; and in the Hereafter he will be in the ranks of those who have lost (all spiritual good).**
>
> *(Sūra 3: Āl-i-ʿImrān, verse: 85)*

These texts and doctrines highlight that exclusivism is not merely a peripheral belief but a central tenet deeply embedded in the theological frameworks of these faiths.

## 2.4 RELIGIOUS INCLUSIVISM:

Religious inclusivism offers a perspective that contrasts with exclusivism by suggesting that while truth is singular, it is expressed through the diverse teachings of various religions. According to this view, each religion reveals a part of the overall truth, with their scriptures and prophets offering different facets of the same ultimate reality. These religious traditions are not seen as contradictory but as complementary, each contributing to a broader and more comprehensive understanding of truth.

From an inclusivist perspective, the ultimate spiritual goal across all religions is the same, despite the varying paths they prescribe to reach it. Religions are seen as unique responses to the divine, shaped by different cultures and historical contexts, each with its own approach to guiding humanity toward the truth.

Followers of an inclusivist view may acknowledge and respect the validity of other religions, recognizing them as alternative paths to human happiness and spiritual success. However, they may still maintain that their own faith offers a more complete or direct route to that goal. This approach fosters mutual respect among different religious groups while affirming the primacy of one's own religious tradition.[20]

## 2.5 EVIDENCE SUPPORTING RELIGIOUS INCLUSIVISM FROM THE THREE ABRAHAMIC RELIGIONS

### 2.5.1 IN JUDAISM:

There are teachings within Judaism that suggest that **"all people are righteous in the afterlife and share in its creation."**[21]

### 2.5.2 IN CHRISTIANITY:

Christianity asserts that **"all humans can partake in the attainment of happiness and success—regardless of their beliefs or opinions—and can benefit from the mercy and grace brought about by Christ's sacrifice."**[22]

### 2.5.3 IN ISLAM:

The Qur'an provides a similar perspective, stating:

> **Those who believe (in the Qur'an) and those who follow the Jewish (Scriptures) and the Christians and the Sabians and who believe in God and the last day and work righteousness shall have their reward with their Lord; on them shall be no fear nor shall they grieve.**
>
> *(Sūra 2: Baqar, verse: 62)*

---

20  Majallat Al-Tawhid (1997). Issue (87)"Al-Ta'addudiyyah Al-Diniyyah: Nazrah Tahliliyyah" by Muhammad Ridha Al-Hijazi,
21  Neusner, Jacob. Judaism: The Evidence of the Mishnah. Fortress Press, 1981.
22  The New Testament, John 3:16; Romans 5:18

In summary, these teachings highlight that religious pluralism is a departure from the previous concepts of exclusivism and inclusivism. The core idea of religious pluralism suggests that each religion has its own independent path to achieving happiness and truth. Since all religions ultimately seek the same goal and aim to reach the same truth, they are all seen as equally valid. In this framework, religions are viewed as different paths, or languages, leading to a single ultimate reality. Thus, all religions can be considered true in their respective ways.[23] The

## 2.6 THE BIBLICAL VIEW AND ITS STANCE ON RELIGIOUS PLURALISM:

Biblical view on religious pluralism has been significantly influenced by the writings of philosophers such as John Hick, who advocated for a broader understanding of truth across different religions. Hick proposed that religious pluralism could serve as a pathway to mutual understanding and harmony among diverse faiths. He used an analogy from the history of astronomy to illustrate his point. He compared the traditional view of religions, where each faith is seen as the center of truth, to the outdated belief that the Earth was the center of the universe. Just as this was later corrected with the understanding that the Earth orbits the Sun, Hick suggested that religious truth should not be confined to a singular, exclusive path but recognized as something that all religions are striving toward in their own ways.

Hick's argument points to the idea that the diversity of religious beliefs is not an obstacle but rather an essential feature of the search for ultimate truth. He contends that viewing religious pluralism in this

---

23  ibid (53). Also see: Islamic Knowledge Journal, The International Institute for Islamic Thought, Year 1, Issue 2, Rabi' al-Akhir 1416H - September 1995, an article on the intellectual position of Ibn Rushd between the West and Islam, by Muhammad Amara. In it, the author states that Ibn Rushd was one of those who advocated for the unity of truth, not its duality. That is, the essence of truth is one in itself, and it is the Divine Self; the multiplicity is in the ways of approaching this single truth or in the details of the knowledge held by each group of people about the one truth (pp. 105-111).

light allows for a more inclusive perspective—one that recognizes the validity of different religious paths while also acknowledging a shared goal: the pursuit of spiritual truth. This inclusive approach, according to Hick, can foster greater tolerance and appreciation among different religious communities, allowing them to coexist more peacefully and productively.[24]

## 2.7 THE FIRST ISLAMIC PERSPECTIVE:

This perspective asserts that Islam views other religions through an exclusivist lens. In an article published in *Al-Tawheed* magazine on Islam and religious pluralism, Dr. Mohamed Legenhousem, who critiqued Hick's ideas through his religious writings, explains the Islamic stance on the issue of religious pluralism. He states:

"The criticisms of the religious pluralism concept embraced by Hick can be summarized in the following points:

First, this concept of religious pluralism, at first glance, appears to promote religious tolerance or peaceful coexistence. However, in reality, it distorts other beliefs to eliminate the fundamental and essential differences between them.

Second, it assumes that the conflicts between adherents of different religions are more related to doctrine than to practical matters, thereby neglecting the religious importance of legislation and community.

Third, by downplaying doctrinal disagreements, it weakens the influence of religious authority.

Fourth, it undermines the use of reason as a tool for achieving greater religious understanding and resolving conflicts, contradicting the reality that rational debate has been central to all doctrinal and cultural discussions in the major world religions.

---

24  Hick, John. Truth and Dialogue in World Religions. Westminster Press, 1974, p. 30. See also : Hick, John. Problems of Religious Pluralism. St. Martin's Press, 1985, p. 34.

Fifth, it presents religious mysticism as a means of acquiring personal religious experiences[25], which may lead to the development of other beliefs. Since this idea seeks to establish a Protestant liberalism, it is seen as foreign to religions, especially Islam.

Sixth, it assumes the correctness of the modern liberal political system, which is incompatible with the religious values upheld by the world's religions as understood by their followers throughout history"[26].

Dr. Mohamed Legenhousem continues to emphasize that Islam's view of other religions is one of religious exclusivism, and he supports this with several Quranic verses. He argues:

## 2.7.1 EXCLUSIVITY IN THE PATH OF TRUTH:

If we were to allow both monotheism and polytheism to each chart their own course, as Hick suggests, how can we explain the Quranic story about Ibrahim, where he broke the idols and destroyed them? Why did Ibrahim not allow polytheism to persist alongside monotheism on Earth? Is there any justification for his act of destruction? Was the purpose of his message simply that he did not find idol worship appropriate for his time and place?[27]

## 2.7.2 ISLAMIC EXCLUSIVISM:

Islam's perspective on other religions is one of exclusivity. Allah, in His wisdom, has decreed Islam as the only true religion for His creation. There is no other true faith that people should follow except Islam. This is why all the prophets and messengers carried with them the concept of Islam, with its core principle being the doctrine of monotheism.[28]

---

25  Arkon, Muhammad. Nafidhah 'ala al-Islam. Translated by Sayah al-Jahim, Dar Atiyah for Publishing, 1996, pp. 127-134.

26  Al-T-. Foundation of Islamic Thought. "Al-Tawheed: A Quarterly Journal of Islamic Thought and Culture," vol. 14, no. 3, Fall 1997, pp. 121-129. Islamic Republic of Iran, 1997.

27  Ibid : P.129

28  Ibid : P.130

### 2.7.3 VALIDITY OF PREVIOUS MESSAGES:

This does not mean that the messages brought by previous prophets were wrong; far from it. They were also divine messages. However, their scope was limited in terms of time and place, unlike the message of Muhammad ﷺ, which is universal and applicable to all times and places.[29]

### 2.7.4 QURANIC EVIDENCE FOR EXCLUSIVISM:

There are several Quranic verses that indicate the exclusivist view of Islam towards other religions.[30] For example, Allah says:

- " **The same religion has He Established for you as that Which He enjoined on Noah–The which We have sent By inspiration to thee–And that which We enjoined On Abraham, Moses, and Jesus : Namely, that ye should remain Steadfast in Religion, and make No divisions therein :** (Sūra 42: Shūra, verse:13)

- "**Those who deny God and his Apostles and (those who) wish to separate God from His Apostles saying: "We believe in some but reject others": and (those who) wish to take a course midway." "They are in truth (equally) unbelievers; and We have prepared for unbelievers a humiliating punishment".** (Sūra 4: Nisāa, verses:150-151)

- "**It is He Who hath sent His Apostle with Guidance And the Religion of Truth, To proclaim it Over all religion, Even though the Pagans May detest (it).** (Sūra 9: Tauba, verse: 33)

- "**We have not sent thee But as a universal (Messenger) To men, giving them Glad tidings, and warning them (Against sin), but most men Understand not. (Sūra 34: Sabā, verse:28)**

- " **O ye who believe! believe in God and his Apostle and the scripture which He hath sent to His Apostle and the scripture which He sent to those before (him). And who denieth God His angels His Books His Apostles and the Day of Judgment hath gone far far astray. (Sūra 4: Nisāa, verses: 136)**

---

29  Ibid : P.130
30  Ibid : P.132-133

## 2.7.8 HICK'S ACKNOWLEDGMENT:

John Hick himself admits that the idea of religious pluralism is not compatible with the nature of Islam, as Muslims believe in the centrality of Islam and that Muhammad is the Seal of the Prophets. Therefore, followers of other religions must ultimately accept this truth and follow this path. Hick concludes, "This conviction among Muslims is what prevents the idea of religious pluralism from finding a foothold within Islamic thought."

It is evident that the writer attempts to prove the exclusivist view of Islam through his critiques of Hick and by referencing Quranic verses that emphasize the universality of the Prophet Muhammad's message. According to this view, there can be no other religion that its followers could claim as a legitimate path to salvation, apart from Islam.

## 2.8 THE SECOND ISLAMIC PERSPECTIVE:

## 2.8.1 RELIGIOUS PLURALISM AS A QURANIC AND PROPHETIC PRINCIPLE:

This perspective posits that Islam's view of other religions embraces the concept of religious pluralism. While the Islamic stance on this topic is multifaceted, this particular view argues for the validity of religious pluralism, drawing on evidence from the **Qur'an**, the **Prophetic traditions**, historical context, and scholarly interpretations. The argument is grounded in seven main themes[31]:

## 2.8.2 THE UNIVERSALITY AND MULTIPLICITY OF DIVINE MESSAGES

This perspective emphasizes that Allah ﷻ is not exclusively the deity of Muslims but the Creator and Sustainer of all humanity. His divine

---

31  Aslan, Adam. "Islam and Religious Diversity." The Islamic Quarterly, Vol. XXXX, No. 3rd Quarter, 1416/1996, Islamic Culture Center, London, p. 173.

guidance has reached all peoples, across time and space, as evidenced by numerous Quranic verses:

- **"To God belong the East and the West; whithersoever ye turn there is the presence of God. For God is All-Pervading All-Knowing"** (Sūra2, verse: Baqara, *115*)

- **"For We assuredly sent Amongst every People an apostle, (With the Command), " Serve God, and eschew Evil " "** *(Sūra 16: Nahl, verse:16:36)*

- **"Verily We have sent thee In truth, as a bearer Of glad tidings, And as a warner : And there never was A people, without a warner Having lived among them (In the past).** (Sūra 35: Fātir, verse:24)

- **"Apostles who gave good news as well as warning that mankind after (the coming) of the Apostles should have no plea against God: for God is Exalted in Power, Wise."** (Sūra 4: Nisāa, verse:165)

These verses collectively affirm that no community was left without divine guidance, suggesting that every faith tradition has its own unique path to spiritual fulfillment and success. While differences may exist in the approaches to truth, the ultimate goal remains singular: the pursuit of human salvation and divine approval.

## 2.8.3 DIVERSITY AS A MANIFESTATION OF DIVINE MERCY

The diversity of races, nations, languages, and religions is viewed as a natural and divinely intended phenomenon, reflecting Allah's wisdom and mercy. This perspective sees pluralism as integral to the fabric of creation[32], as articulated in the Qur'an:

> **O mankind ! We created You from a single (pair) Of a male and a female, And made you into Nations and tribes, that Ye may know each other (Not that ye may despise Each other). Verily The most honoured of you In the sight of God Is (he who is) the most Righteous of**

---

32   Ibid, P.74

**you. And God has full knowledge And is well acquainted (With all things).**

*(Sūra 49: Hujurāt,verse:13)* 🙶

Here, diversity is not seen as a source of division but as an opportunity for mutual understanding and cooperation among different groups of people.

## 2.8.4 ISLAM AS SUBMISSION TO ALLAH ﷻ, BEYOND LABELS

Islam, in its linguistic and theological essence, signifies submission to Allah ﷻ.[33] This submission is not confined to the adherents of a single religious system but extends to all who turn to Allah ﷻ with sincerity, regardless of their formal religious affiliation. For example:

- The Qur'an describes Prophet Ibrahim (Abraham) as: "**Abraham was not a Jew nor yet a Christian but he was true in faith and bowed his will to God's (which is Islam) and he joined not gods with God**" (Sūra 3: Āl-i-'Imrān, verse:*67)*

- Similarly, the prayer of Ibrahim and his son Ismail includes: "**Our Lord! make of us Muslims bowing to Thy (Will) and of our progeny a people Muslim bowing to Thy (Will).**" (Sūra 2: Baqara, verse:128)

This understanding expands the term "Muslim" to include anyone who sincerely submits to the will of Allah ﷻ, irrespective of their specific religious identity, emphasizing a shared spiritual essence among monotheistic traditions.[34]

## 2.8.5 FREEDOM OF RELIGION – "NO COMPULSION IN FAITH"

The Qur'anic principle of **religious freedom** is firmly established in the verse:

---

33  Ibid, P.175

34  Hick, J., & Askari, H. (1985). The Experience of Religious Diversity. Aldershot and Brookfield: Gower, p. 199.

"**Let there be no compulsion in religion. Truth stands out clear from error;.**"*(Sūra 2: Baqara, verse:256)*

This verse articulates the idea that faith cannot and should not be forced. Each individual has the autonomy to follow their own religious path and practice their beliefs. Coercion into embracing Islam is neither valid nor acceptable. Supporting this are additional verses:

- **" Say, " The Truth is From your Lord " : Let him who will, Believe, and let him Who will, reject (it)."** (Sūra 18: Kahf, verse:29).

- **" If it had been the Lord's Will, They would all have believed,— All who are on earth ! Wilt thou then compel mankind, Against their will, to believe"** (Sūra 10: Yūnus,verse:99)

## 2.8.6 INCLUSIVITY IN QURANIC VERSES ON RELIGION

Some Qur'anic verses that are often interpreted as exclusive to Islam are argued to support a broader, pluralistic view. For instance, the verse:

- **The Religion before God is Islam (submission to His will)."** (Sūra 3: Āl-i-'Imrān, verse:19)

In this context, *Islam* can be understood linguistically as "submission to Allah ﷻ," rather than the institutionalized religion. This interpretation broadens the meaning to include anyone who surrenders sincerely to God, free from idolatry, regardless of their specific religious affiliation. Such an interpretation is echoed by scholars like Sheikh al-Maghribi, who emphasize the universality of submission to God[35].

## 2.8.7 THE THREE CRITERIA FOR SALVATION

According to this perspective, the Qur'an outlines three fundamental criteria for achieving salvation and escaping eternal punishment:

1. **Faith in Allah ﷻ**

2. **Belief in the Last Day**

3. **Righteous deeds**

---

35  The Islamic Quarterly, Vol. XXXX, No. 3rd Quarter, 1416/1996, p. 175

These principles are universal and not confined to any specific religious identity. This inclusivity is supported by verses like:

- **"Those who believe (in the Qur'an) and those who follow the Jewish (Scriptures) and the Christians and the Sabians and who believe in God and the last day and work righteousness shall have their reward with their Lord; on them shall be no fear nor shall they grieve."** *(Sūra 2: Baqara, verse:62)*

Another verse reinforces the reward for good deeds and belief:

> **Whoever works righteousness, Man or woman, and has Faith, Verily, to him will We give A new Life, a life That is good and pure, and We Will bestow on such their reward According to the best Of their actions.**
>
> (Sūra 16: Nahl, verse:97)

This perspective challenges the notion that salvation is exclusive to Islam, contrasting it with certain Christian doctrines that assert salvation can only be attained through the Church[36]. Ismail Raji al-Faruqi emphasized that Islam's respect for Judaism and Christianity goes beyond mere courtesy, reflecting a recognition of the religious truths they embody. He argued that Islam does not view these faiths as foreign ideologies but acknowledges them as divinely revealed religions. Furthermore, he highlighted that Islam uniquely requires belief in other revealed religions as a core component of its theological framework.[37]

## 2.8.8 HISTORICAL PRECEDENTS OF COEXISTENCE

Islam's historical record of peaceful treaties and coexistence with other religions provides strong evidence of its recognition of other faiths and their spiritual destinies without undue interference. These

---

36  Ibid, 178

37  Faruqi, I. R. (1989). Toward a Critical World Theology. In Towards Islamization of Disciplines. Heidon: International Institute of Islamic Thought, pp. 435-436.

precedents reflect the Qur'anic ethos of allowing each community to follow its own path toward spiritual fulfillment.

## 2.8.9 CONCLUSION: THE PLURALISTIC ESSENCE OF ISLAM

This perspective concludes that each religion has its own independent path to achieving happiness and salvation. This understanding is deeply rooted in the spirit of the Qur'an, which emphasizes:

1. Adherence to the moral and spiritual values of one's faith.

2. Avoiding the suppression of religious truths due to fear of persecution or societal pressure.

The renowned Islamic scholar Rashid Rida supported this pluralistic view, emphasizing the core principles of faith shared across divine messages:

1. Belief in Allah ﷻ.

2. Faith in the Day of Judgment.

3. Commitment to righteous deeds[38].

Rashid Rida argued that any follower of a revealed religion who sincerely fulfills these criteria is promised salvation, as indicated by:

- **"Those who believe (in the Qur'an) and those who follow the Jewish (Scriptures) and the Christians and the Sabians and who believe in God and the last day and work righteousness shall have their reward with their Lord; on them shall be no fear nor shall they grieve."** *(Sūra 2: Baqara, verse:62)*

In his tafsir, Rida also highlighted the legitimacy of uprightness among the People of the Book, even when they remain within their original faith traditions, as long as their practice reflects sincerity and adherence to the core truths revealed to them.[39]

---

38  The Islamic Quarterly, Vol. XXXX, No. 3rd Quarter, 1416/1996, p. 179

39  Tafsir al-Manar, 1/112, https://www.noor-book.com-pdf

## 2.9 DISCUSSION OF THESE VIEWS:

Issuing an academic judgment on the concept of **"religious pluralism"** requires a comprehensive understanding of the foundational principles and ideas underlying the concept. It is essential to interpret the Qur'an and Hadith in light of the essence of Islam, and in accordance with its correct understanding as the true religion that came to complete the other preceding faiths. While Islam may accept aspects of this concept, as implied by certain verses, this does not mean unconditional acceptance. Therefore, there are several critiques of this idea, alongside the points raised by Muhammad Liegnusam in his response to Hick:

**First:** The establishment of Islam as a religion by the Creator, presenting the new faith as the most complete, negates the legitimacy and validity of the previous religions coexisting alongside the new one during the same period.

**Second:** Even if the truth of both religions is rooted in the same source of divine emanation, this very truth negates the legitimacy and right of the previous faith to continue once the new religion has arrived.

**Third:** The success and happiness sought by all is now found in the new religion. Therefore, the lawgiver calls everyone to follow this new faith because it is the most complete of all the religions brought by the prophets who preceded it, from Adam to Moses and Jesus.

**Fourth:** God's statement, **"If anyone desires a religion other than Islam (submission to God) never will it be accepted of him; and in the Hereafter he will be in the ranks of those who have lost (all spiritual good).** (Sūra 3: Āl-i-'Imrān, verse:85). This understanding of Islam, based on the Qur'an and Hadith, is fundamentally incompatible with the core principles of religious pluralism; accepting one religion implies rejecting the others.

**Fifth:** Assuming for argument's sake that this idea holds some merit, why do its proponents call for dialogue among different religious groups? If everyone's faith is correct, what is the point of interfaith dialogue? What about the numerous verses in the Qur'an urging Muslims to engage in dialogue with the People of the Book? Why did the Qur'an itself argue with the People of the Book and engage in dialogue with them? Why would God call Muslims to do something that contradicts reality in all its dimensions? This contradiction reinforces the concept of religious exclusivism advocated by Islam.[40]

## 2.10 RESPONSES TO THE ARGUMENTS PRESENTED BY THOSE SUPPORTING THE IDEA OF RELIGIOUS PLURALISM:

### 2.10.1 THE "UNIVERSALITY OF DIVINE MESSAGES"

The **"universality of divine messages"** is undoubtedly a Qur'anic truth that cannot be denied. However, these verses only indicate that Allah ﷻ sent a messenger to every nation to prevent any excuse for people after the messengers. These divine messages were only valid for a limited period of time, and since their validity is no longer ongoing, the final and comprehensive message has arrived, which encompasses all the unifying factors and elements connecting the divine messages. In this final message, the fundamental beliefs and actions of the religion are clearly laid out, and it also offers an account of the nations and their responses to the faith as conveyed by the messengers.

### 2.10.2 THE "DIVERSITY OF RACES, PEOPLES, AND COLORS"

The **"diversity of races, peoples, and colors"** is indeed a sign of God's mercy, as well as a miraculous manifestation of His creative power. Although this diversity originates from a single source, it reflects the diversity within God's creation. However, this diversity does not imply the existence of multiple creators; God remains the one Creator. Since He is the source of the one religious truth, the true religion remains singular, not plural or fragmented. This unified understanding is consistent with the calls of all the prophets.

---

40  Majallat at-Tawḥīd, al-'Adad 87, as-Sanah al-Khāmah 'Asharah, Dhū al-Qa'dah 1417H - Mārch 1997M (ṣ. 56)

## 2.10.3 "ISLAM IS REFERRED TO AS THE NAME FOR ALL DIVINE RELIGIONS".

The message of Muhammad ﷺ calls for the realization of this concept of Islam. However, the claim that Abraham was Jewish or Christian does not prevent the People of the Book and others, if they surrender to God in obedience and submission, from being counted among the Muslims. True submission is what leads them to recognize the singular religious truth upheld by Muslims and the legitimacy of the message of Muhammad ﷺ.

## 2.10.4 THE QUR'ANIC VERSE, "LET THERE BE NO COMPULSION IN RELIGION.

**Truth stands out clear from error;** " (Sūra 2: Baqara, verse: 256), instructs Muslims not to force others to join their faith but to invite them to it, allowing them to accept the truth voluntarily once it is clearly conveyed. Compulsion contradicts the nature of Islamic preaching, which relies on mercy, reason, and logical argument to win over hearts. Historically, coercion was never a means for spreading Islam, but rather, Muslims were known for their noble character, which made their message resonate with others.

The verse **" Say, " The Truth is From your Lord " : Let him who will, Believe, and let him Who will, reject (it)"** (Sūra 18: Kahf, verse: 29) confirms that the truth is one, and by believing in this singular truth, a person is a believer, while rejecting it makes them a disbeliever. This supports the notion of religious exclusivism, wherein those who follow Islam are true believers and those who reject it are disbelievers.

**Fifth:** The verse **"The Religion before God is Islam (submission to His will):"** (Sura 3: Āl-i-'Imrān, verse: 19) directly supports the concept of religious exclusivism. While alternative interpretations might suggest the verse points to pluralism, the plain meaning affirms that Islam is the sole true religion. Hence, any attempts to interpret it as supporting pluralism contradict the original and clear understanding.

## 2.10.5 "THE BASIC CONDITIONS..."

The established principle among interpreters is that the Qur'an explains itself. When a meaning is generalized in one verse, there is often another verse that provides a more detailed explanation. This applies to the verses cited by the author. Thus, it is not logically sound to cite one aspect while neglecting the other, as the general statement's meaning is not complete unless clarified by its detailed counterpart.

Some of the verses that support the intended meaning of faith in these verses are as follows:

1.  **The verse: "O ye people of the Book! believe in what We have (now) revealed confirming what was (already) with you before We change the face and fame of some (of you) beyond all recognition and turn them hindwards or curse them as We cursed the Sabbath-breakers: for the decision of God must be carried out."** (Sūra 4: Nisāa, versr: 47).

This verse clearly demands that the People of the Book believe in what was sent down to Muhammad, which is Islam. This represents the essence of the faith referred to in these verses.

2.  **The verse: "O ye who believe! believe in God and his Apostle and the scripture which He hath sent to His Apostle and the scripture which He sent to those before (him). And who denieth God His angels His Books His Apostles and the Day of Judgment hath gone far far astray. "**(Sūra 4: Nisāa, verse: 136).

3.  **The verse: ". *Say: "O People of the Book! ye have no ground to stand upon unless ye stand fast by the Law the Gospel and all the revelation that has come to you from your Lord." It is the revelation that cometh to thee from thy Lord that increaseth in most of them their obstinate rebellion and blasphemy. But sorrow thou not over (these) people without Faith."* (Sūra 5: Māida, verse: 68).**

This verse calls upon the People of the Book to uphold the scriptures sent to them, and such an act implies belief in the message of Muhammad, which is outlined in their own books.

Sayed Qutb explains the verse **"Those who believe (in the Qur'an) and those who follow the Jewish (Scriptures) and the Christians and the Sabians and who believe in God and the last day and work righteousness shall have their reward with their Lord; on them shall be no fear nor shall they grieve."** (Sūra 2: Baqara, verse: 62) as follows:

> 66 The verse asserts that whatever the sect, if they believed in Allah and the Last Day and did righteous deeds – and implicitly, as stated in other verses, this was done in accordance with the teachings brought by the final messenger – then they have been saved: *'They will have no fear, nor will they grieve.'* This applies not only to the Jews and Christians but to anyone who follows the core truth as prescribed by the final revelation."[41] 99

As for what Professor Ismail Raja Faruqi pointed out, it is an undisputed fact that Islam recognizes the existence of these two religions (Judaism and Christianity) as prior Abrahamic faiths, and that it obliges its followers to truly believe in them. This belief in these faiths is a fundamental component of Islamic faith, for these religions brought forth the truth which Islam, as the religion of Ibrahim (Abraham peace be upon him) and Muhammad (ﷺ), affirms. However, what the author misunderstood in Faruqi's statements is not that Islam is not the final and complete religion, but rather that it recognizes the respect due to these faiths and their followers, especially as they are closer in their teachings to Islam than other religions. This respect forms the foundation for interfaith dialogue aimed at correcting misunderstandings and restoring truth to the distorted concepts of these religions.[42]

Sayed Qutb, in his explanation of *"Not all of them are alike: of the People of the book are a portion that stand (for the right); they rehearse the signs of God all night long and then prostrate themselves in adoration.")* (Sūra 3: Āl-i-'Imrān, verse: 113), describes a positive portrayal of those among the People of the Book who embraced true

---

41  Fi Ẓilāl al-Qur'ān (2/942)
42  Ibid, 1/450

faith and joined the Muslim community. He asserts that their genuine belief in Allah and the principles outlined by the last Prophet led them to Islam, which they saw as the fulfillment of what had been mentioned in their own scriptures.

It is also important to note that although the interpretation of verses often relies on the general meaning rather than the context of revelation[43], it is still permissible to consider the original context in order to fully understand the intended meaning of a verse. In the case of the verse, it was revealed concerning specific individuals like Abdullah ibn Salam and others who converted to Islam and were praised by Allah ﷻ for their true belief in the Islamic faith. Their conversion faced opposition from their own people who regarded them as the worst among them, saying, "Only the worst among us believed in Muhammad, had they been the best, they would not have abandoned their forefathers' faith."[44]

The Al-Bahr Al-Muheet states: "Belief in the Last Day inherently includes belief in the prophets, as they were the ones who foretold of this possibility, making belief in the afterlife a necessity."[45]

## 2.10.6 "HISTORICAL EVIDENCE..."

What history has affirmed is the true system of Islam, founded on justice and the respect for human rights. It embodies principles of respect, good neighborliness, and a love for the well-being of all, as Islam commands its followers. However, the tolerance witnessed throughout history was not based on principles that contradict the inclusivity and universality of Islam. This message echoes a resounding call, reverberating in every time and place **"The Religion before God is Islam (submission to His will)."** (Sūra 3: Āl-i-'Imrān, verse: 19).

Moreover, this tolerance did not come at the expense of religion, where Muslims would relinquish their faith or their rightful claim to the

---

43  Zaydān, Dr. ʿAbd al-Karīm. Al-Wujayz fī Uṣūl al-Fiqh. Al-Risālah Foundation, Beirut, 1st edition, 1415 AH - 1994 CE, p. 324.
44  Tafsir Āl-i-'Imrān, verse: 113https://alsunniah.com/search/content?query
45  Tafsīr al-Baḥr al-Muḥīṭ. Vol. 3, p. 38.

eternal message. The Islamic call was vigorously spread across the entire inhabited world, engaging with people of all religions, yet always within the boundaries of respect and consideration for the feelings of others. All treaties and agreements signed with the People of the Book or others were in favor of the Islamic mission. In such peaceful conditions, Muslims were able to present their message and engage in religious discussions with others on many matters of faith.

If the concept of **"religious pluralism"** were truly an acceptable one, why did these people not abandon their beliefs? The call was not to impose a narrow religious perspective, but rather to express a form of religious inclusivism, one characterized by its fundamental aim: the straight path of Islam.

The broader concept of pluralism, unbound by a specific religious framework, seeks to establish democratic principles and open the door to freedom. However, it also opens the door to chaos, fear, and confusion. Since this concept aligns with Western agendas and facilitates their control, it has garnered significant attention from outsiders and their followers. This has led to increased discussions about it, amplifying its value and elevating its importance.

# 3.0 CONCLUSION

All praise is due to Allah ﷻ, through whose blessings all righteous deeds are completed. Praise and gratitude also belong to Him for His visible and invisible graces, and peace and blessings be upon the Messenger of Allah.

**Key Findings:** Through the pages of this study, several important conclusions have been drawn, among the most significant of which are:

1. **The Abrahamic Faith and Islam**: The Abrahamic faith is, in its true sense, Islam, which requires complete submission and total obedience to the will of Allah ﷻ. It is the Islam brought by Prophet Muhammad ﷺ as revealed to him by his Lord. Its true name is Islam, and its followers are thus Muslims, as indicated in the Qur'an: **"It is He Who has named You Muslims, both before And in this (Revelation)"** (Sūra 22: Hajj, verse:78).

2. **True Belonging to the Faith**: Genuine affiliation with this religion is realized through the method of Prophet Ibrahim (Abraham) and his relationship with Allah ﷻ, which was embodied by Prophet Muhammad ﷺ in his conduct and life.

3. **Monotheism of the Abrahamic Religion**: There is only one Abrahamic religion, despite the different names and laws of its followers. The truth is singular, as it has one source, one purpose, and one goal.

4. **Islamic Perspective on Religious Pluralism**: The correct Islamic view on pluralism in paths to truth and salvation is exclusive, meaning that Islam is the correct path through which one achieves salvation and is granted deliverance.

5. **Openness to Dialogue**: Despite Islam being the true and final religion, abrogating previous ones, this does not prevent Islam from being open to dialogue with other religions. Constructive discussions among followers of various faiths can contribute to peaceful coexistence and mutual respect.

# 4.0 RECOMMENDATIONS

1. Conducting academic research on this topic, adhering to a methodological and objective approach, based on authentic evidence from the Qur'an and Sunnah.

2. Warning against placing reason above revelation when discussing theological matters, particularly those related to interfaith comparisons.

3. Fostering discussions on issues of pluralism and absolute truth among academics specializing in theology and comparative religion.

4. Translating works in other languages on this subject into Arabic, as there is a shortage of Arabic sources, with only scattered articles in journals and newspapers available.

# 5.0 REFERENCES

## REFERENCES IN ARABIC

- Al-Aqqad, A. M. (n.d.). *Ibrahim Abu al-Anbiya*. Al-Maktabah al-'Asriyah, Beirut.

- Al-Alouri, A. A. (1988). *Tārīkh al-Da'wah Bayn al-Amās wa al-Yawm* (3rd ed.). Dar al-Tadāmun Press, Cairo.

- Al-Khalidi, S. (1994). *Haqqā'iq Qur'āniyah ḥawla al-Qadiyah al-Filasṭīniyah*. Palestine Muslim Publications, London.

- Al-Sousa, A. (1972). *Mufassal al-'Arab wa al-Yahūd fi al-Tārīkh*. Ministry of Information Publications, Baghdad, Iraq.

- Al-Zaydān, A. (1994). *Al-Wajīz fi Uṣūl al-Fiqh* (1st ed.). Maktabat al-Risālah, Beirut.

- Haroun, A. (1981). *Tahdheeb Sīrat Ibn Hishām* (8th ed.). Beirut, Lebanon.

- Arkoun, M. (1996). *Nāfidah 'ala al-Islām* ('Trans. S. Al-Juhaim). Dar Atiyah, Beirut, Lebanon.

- *Tafsīr al-Baḥr al-Muḥīt* (n.d.). Beirut, Lebanon: Dar al-Kutub al-'Ilmiyyah.

- *Al-Tafsīr al-Munīr fi al-'Aqīdah wa al-Sharī'ah wa al-Manhaj* (n.d.). Beirut, Lebanon: Dar al-Fikr al-Mu'āṣir.

- *Majallat al-Tawḥīd* (1997). No. 87, Vol. 15, Dhul-Qa'dah 1417 AH - March.

- *Majallat al-Islāmīyah al-Ma'rifah* (1995). Al-Ma'had al-'Ālamī li al-Fikr al-Islāmī, Vol. 1, No. 2, Rabī' al-Ākhir 1416 AH - September.

- Qutb, S. (1987). *Fi Ẓilāl al-Qur'ān* (13th ed.). Cairo: Dar al-Shurūq.

## ONLINE SOURCES

- **Tafsir al-Manar:** Rashid Rida, Muhammad. Tafsir al-Manar. Vol. 1, p. 112. Noor Book, *https://www.noor-book.com-pdf*.
- **Tafsir Āl-i-ʿImrān, Verse 113**: "Tafsir Āl-i-ʿImrān, Verse 113." Al-Sunniah, *https://alsunniah.com/search/content?query*.

## REFERENCES IN ENGLISH

- Aslan, A. (1996). "Islam and Religious Diversity." *The Islamic Quarterly*, 40(3), 1416. London: Islamic Culture Center.
- Centre for the Study of Islam & Christian Muslim Relations. (1997). "Islam and Christian Muslim Relations," 8(2), July.
- Daidies, S. (1910). *The Jews in Babylonia*. London: London Press.
- Faruqi, I. R. (1989). "Toward a Critical World Theology." In *Towards Islamization of Disciplines*. Heidon: International Institute of Islamic Thought.
- Foundation of Islamic Thought. (1997). "Al-Tawheed: A Quarterly Journal of Islamic Thought and Culture," 14(3), Fall. Tehran: Islamic Republic of Iran.
- Hick, J. (1974). *Truth and Dialogue in World Religions*. Philadelphia: Westminster Press.
- Hick, J. (1985). *Problems of Religious Pluralism*. New York: St. Martin's Press.
- Hick, J., & Askari, H. (1985). *The Experience of Religious Diversity*. Aldershot and Brookfield: Gower.
- Islamic Culture Centre. (1996). *Islamic Quarterly*, 40(3), 3rd Quarter, 1410. London: Islamic Culture Centre.
- Patai, R. (1986). *The Seed of Abraham: Jews and Arabs in Contact and Conflict*. Salt Lake City: University of Utah Press.

# PART
# 2

# THE ABRAHAMIC DIALOGUE PROJECT BETWEEN JUDAISM, CHRISTIANITY, AND ISLAM:

## *A Critical Reading of the Issues, Objectives, and Obstacles of the Initiative*

## DR. ALI MOHAMED SALAH

## ABSTRACT

This research aims to provide a critical analysis of the Abrahamic dialogue initiative between the three Abrahamic faiths (Islam, Christianity, and Judaism), focusing on the issues, challenges, and objectives surrounding the project. The study critically examines the Abrahamic project as a unifying religious framework—as its proponents claim—seeking to integrate the Abrahamic religions alongside some non-Abrahamic faiths under a unified religious umbrella called "the Abrahamic religion." While the project is presented as a means to promote global peace, deepen understanding among followers of different religions, and resolve conflicts, it raises concerns about restricting freedom of belief and reshaping religious identity. The research discusses the challenges facing the implementation of this project in Islamic countries, amid what many perceive as attempts to impose a unified religion that conflicts with original religious teachings and interferes with religious freedom. It also highlights the political and social aspects of this initiative, including its impact on educational curricula, where some institutions have begun to remove religious studies and replace them with ethics education, reflecting a shift in educational approaches. Overall, the research seeks to analyze the obstacles to the implementation of the

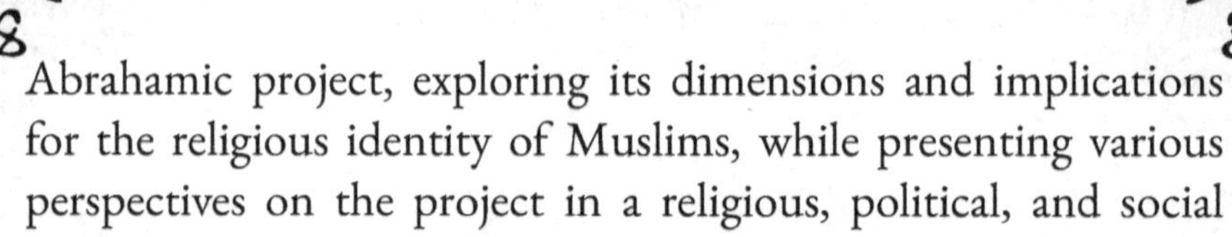

Abrahamic project, exploring its dimensions and implications for the religious identity of Muslims, while presenting various perspectives on the project in a religious, political, and social context.

# ملخص البحث

يهدف هذا البحث إلى تقديم قراءة نقدية لمبادرة الحوار الإبراهيمي بين الأديان السماوية الثلاثة (الإسلام، المسيحية، اليهودية)، مع التركيز على الإشكاليات والتحديات والأهداف التي تحيط بالمشروع. تناقش الدراسة وبرؤية نقدية المشروع الإبراهيمي كإطار ديني توحيدي — كما يزعم أصحابه —، يسعى إلى دمج الديانات الإبراهيمية جنبًا إلى جنب مع بعض الأديان غير الإبراهيمية تحت مظلة دينية موحدة تُسمى «الدين الإبراهيمي». وبينما يُقدَّم المشروع كوسيلة لتعزيز السلام العالمي، وتعميق التفاهم بين أتباع الأديان المختلفة، والعمل على حل النزاعات، فإنه يثير مخاوف حول مصادرة حرية الاعتقاد وإعادة تشكيل الهوية الدينية.

يناقش البحث التحديات التي يواجهها تنفيذ هذا المشروع في الدول الإسلامية، في ظل ما يعتبره الكثيرون محاولات لفرض دين موحد يتعارض مع التعاليم الدينية الأصلية، ويتداخل مع حرية الاعتقاد. كما يسلط الضوء على المظاهر السياسية والاجتماعية لهذه المبادرة، بما في ذلك تأثيرها على مناهج التعليم، حيث بدأت بعض المؤسسات بإزالة مواد الدين واستبدالها بتعليم الأخلاق، وهو ما يعكس تحولاً في الأساليب التربوية.

يسعى البحث في مجمله إلى تحليل العقبات التي تقف في وجه تطبيق المشروع الإبراهيمي، واستكشاف أبعاده وتداعياته على الهوية الدينية للمسلمين، مع عرض المواقف المختلفة من المشروع في سياق ديني وسياسي واجتماعي.

# FOUNDATIONAL OVERVIEW OF THE STUDY:
## OBJECTIVES, MOTIVATION, CHALLENGES, METHODOLOGY, AND FRAMEWORK

**Research Objectives:** The research aims to achieve several objectives, most notably:

- To protect the Islamic creed and religious identity from any attempts to merge it into a new religion or alter it, preserving the constants of the faith and the distinct Islamic identity.

- To shed light on the true intentions behind the Abrahamic Project, which may be linked to political or social agendas seeking to alter religious power dynamics or cultural dominance.

- To reject attempts to assimilate Muslims into a new cultural or religious framework that seeks to diminish their religious uniqueness.

- To affirm the freedom of belief and defend Muslims' right to believe and choose freely, without imposing a new religious model aimed at uniting the Abrahamic faiths under the concept of "Abrahamic religion."

## REASONS FOR CHOOSING THE TOPIC:

- **Alignment with Specialization:** The choice of the topic aligns with the academic specialization concerned with Islamic affairs and interfaith dialogue. This field requires a deep understanding of the doctrinal, cultural, and political dimensions related to the Abrahamic Project and its potential impact on Muslim societies.

- **Need for a Comprehensive Study:** The topic is multidimensional, touching on religious, cultural, social, and political aspects. Thus, conducting a comprehensive study that addresses these various dimensions will provide an integrated perspective, enabling a deeper understanding of the risks and challenges associated with the project.

- **Lack of Academic Research on This Matter:** Despite the growing discourse around the Abrahamic Project, comprehensive and detailed academic studies analyzing this issue from a critical perspective remain limited. This research seeks to fill this academic gap by providing an extensive study that highlights the subject in all its details.

- **Importance of the Topic:** The significance of the topic lies in the contemporary context of the Abrahamic Project, as it is not merely a theoretical idea but an ongoing initiative that seeks implementation in Muslim nations. Therefore, studying this topic is essential for understanding the real challenges facing Muslim communities. Additionally, researching such topics enhances awareness among researchers, decision-makers, and scholars, providing essential information that forms the basis for more comprehensive, profound, and serious research aimed at uprooting the project and safeguarding the nation's faith and creed. This reason, along with the motivations behind this study, makes investigating this topic important for enriching the academic literature related to interfaith dialogue and for understanding the dynamics that may affect the religious identity and culture of Muslims.

- **Previous Studies:** Some of the previous studies that have addressed the Abrahamic Project include:
  - *Al-Hiwar ma'a Ahl al-Kitab fi Daw' al-Qur'an wa al-Sunnah* – Dr. Muhammad Amara
  - *Al-Ibrahimiyya Bayn al-Din wa al-Siyasa: Ru'ya Naqdiyya* – Dr. Saud al-Zamanan
  - *I'adat Ta'areef al-Din: Qira'a Naqdiyya fi Mafhoom al-Din al-Ibrahimiyya* – Dr. Taha Abdul Rahman

- *Al-Mawqif al-Islami min al-Hiwar al-Ibrahimiyya: Diraasa fi al-Huwiyya wa al-Intimaa* – Dr. Yusuf al-Qaradawi

This study contributes to the discourse by focusing on the following aspects:

- The concerns regarding attempts to unify the three Abrahamic religions – analyzing the objectives and challenges

- Offering an Islamic perspective on the obstacles faced by the initiative, particularly from a doctrinal and political viewpoint

- Combining religious analysis of the issues with an exploration of the political factors influencing the dialogue, thus providing a comprehensive perspective.

## THE PROBLEM ADDRESSED BY THE RESEARCH:

The research addresses the issue of assessing the risks and challenges posed by the Abrahamic Project to the Islamic identity and religious doctrine of Muslims. It seeks to shed light on the concerns related to attempts to merge the Abrahamic faiths into a new religion called "Abrahamic Religion" and the potential impact of such efforts on freedom of belief and religious privacy. Additionally, the study aims to analyze the cultural and political aspects of the project, examining how these challenges can be faced from an Islamic perspective that preserves religious independence and protects the core principles of the faith.

## RESEARCH METHODOLOGY:

The research employs a combination of critical and analytical methodologies to provide a comprehensive and integrated view of the Abrahamic Project. By critically evaluating its foundations and analyzing its various dimensions, this approach allows for exploring the potential effects on freedom of belief and the religious identity of Muslims, while offering recommendations on how to address the challenges it presents.

The critical methodology is used to examine and study the concepts and ideas surrounding the Abrahamic Project, including both its explicit and hidden objectives, concerns associated with it, and the challenges it faces. This methodology allows for a critique of the central idea of the project, deconstructing its components to understand the political, social, and religious dimensions that may be driving it.

This includes the following elements:

- Evaluating Obstacles and Challenges: Analyzing the challenges faced by the project in achieving its goals, such as doctrinal and cultural differences between the three Abrahamic religions, and offering recommendations on how to address them.

- Analyzing Discourses and Positions: Studying and analyzing the discourses from both supporters and opponents of the project to understand the real motivations behind this proposal.

- Reviewing Religious and Historical Foundations: Examining the religious and historical roots of the Abrahamic concept, and assessing how well it aligns or conflicts with Islamic teachings.

- Critiquing the Objectives and Policies: Providing a critical reading of both the declared and undeclared goals of the project, and evaluating their potential impact on freedom of belief and religious identity.

## STRUCTURE OF THE RESEARCH

The research is structured into three main sections, followed by a conclusion and recommendations. Below are the key topics covered in the research:

- **First Section:** The Challenges and Concerns Surrounding the Objectives of the Abrahamic Dialogue Project

- **Second Section:** The Challenges to Islamic-Jewish Reconciliation in Achieving the Abrahamic Dialogue Project

- **Third Section:** Challenges to Islamic-Christian Convergence in Realizing the Abrahamic Dialogue Project.

# INTRODUCTION

Praise be to Allah, and may peace and blessings be upon the Messenger of Allah, his family, and his companions. After that:

The introduction of the Abrahamic Project as a unifying religious framework for the three Abrahamic faiths (Islam, Christianity, and Judaism), along with some other religions, has become a source of increasing concern for many Muslims. While the project is presented as an initiative to promote global peace, foster understanding between peoples, and eliminate conflicts, it conceals real dangers that threaten freedom of belief and faith, and it interferes with the nature of religious affiliations. The project seeks to integrate these religions into a unified religious system called the **"Abrahamic Religion,"** selectively drawing moral and behavioral teachings from the holy books (the Qur'an, the Bible, the Torah), while disregarding aspects of Sharia and religious rulings. This, in practice, leads to the marginalization of Islamic Sharia and the rulings of Allah .

In light of these shifts, some international educational institutions have begun removing religious subjects from their curricula and replacing them with ethics classes, reflecting one aspect of this move towards reshaping religious education. Although the concept of the **"Abrahamic Religion"** is not new, its roots go back to the 19th century, when the idea of the "Abrahamic Covenant" was proposed in 1811 to strengthen religious ties in the West. It was later revived by the French scholar Louis Massignon in the mid-20th century through his famous article "The Three Prayers of Abraham, Father of All Believers," published in 1949. Since then, it has evolved into a distinct academic field referred to as "Abrahamic religions."

However, the contemporary political crystallization of this project has sparked widespread debate within Islamic circles, presenting numerous challenges to its implementation in Muslim-majority countries, as many view it as a threat to religious identity and an attempt to reshape it to fit specific agendas.

This researchr aims to analyze these challenges and obstacles by exploring the dimensions of the Abrahamic Project and its implications for the religious identity of Muslims, shedding light on the differing positions towards this project within religious, political, and social contexts.

The author:

Dr. Ali Mohamed Salah

# 1.0 THE CHALLENGES AND CONCERNS SURROUNDING THE OBJECTIVES OF THE ABRAHAMIC DIALOGUE PROJECT

The Abrahamic Dialogue Project aims to foster understanding and cooperation among the followers of Judaism, Christianity, and Islam by emphasizing shared beliefs and values. While such efforts are often viewed as a step toward global harmony, they raise significant questions within the Islamic framework. For Muslims, engaging in dialogue is both a religious duty and an opportunity to share the truth of Islam. However, the project's objectives—particularly notions of "unity among religions"—have sparked theological and philosophical concerns. Examining these challenges is crucial for understanding the boundaries of interfaith engagement in Islamic thought and ensuring that dialogue upholds the integrity of faith and religious identity.

## 1.1 ISLAMIC PERSPECTIVE ON THE OBJECTIVES OF THE ABRAHAMIC DIALOGUE PROJECT:

### 1.1.1 MUSLIM OPENNESS TO DIALOGUE:

Islam encourages dialogue as a means of fostering understanding and sharing truth, provided such exchanges adhere to the principles established by Islamic teachings. Two primary objectives of dialogue align with Islamic values and serve as guiding principles for Muslim participation:

1.  **Correcting Misconceptions About the Religion of Prophet Ibrahim (Abraham):**

    If the Abrahamic Project seeks to dispel misunderstandings surrounding the monotheistic faith of Prophet Ibrahim—who called for the exclusive worship of Allah ﷻ—Islam unequivocally supports such efforts. Engaging in this form of dialogue is not merely permissible; it is a religious obligation. This aligns with Islam's mission to clarify truth, promote monotheism, and guide others toward understanding the worship of the One True God.

2.  **Inviting Jews and Christians to Islam:**

    Dialogue aimed at inviting Jews and Christians to Islam (da'wah) by presenting its virtues and addressing their theological inaccuracies is welcomed. This includes:

    - Exposing distortions and alterations in their scriptures.
    - Highlighting their deviation from the teachings of their prophets.
    - Demonstrating the contradictions inherent in associating partners with Allah.
    - Such dialogue serves as a critical component of the Muslim mission to uphold and propagate the truth of Islam as the final and complete revelation.

### 1.1.2 LIMITS AND CONDITIONS FOR DIALOGUE:

Islamic teachings impose clear boundaries on dialogue. Any initiative that contradicts the principles of Islamic law or undermines its objectives—particularly by compromising the unique position of Islam as the ultimate truth—is impermissible. The concept of "unity among the Abrahamic religions," as presented in the Abrahamic Project, is one such initiative that raises significant concerns.

## 1.1.3 THE PHILOSOPHICAL DIMENSION OF "UNITY AMONG THE ABRAHAMIC RELIGIONS"

The Abrahamic Project promotes the idea that Judaism, Christianity, and Islam collectively share fragments of the truth and together form complementary paths to salvation[46]. This pluralistic notion challenges the exclusivist truth claim of Islam as articulated in the Qur'an. For Muslims, this perspective undermines the finality and completeness of Islam as the divinely chosen faith, as explicitly stated:

**"This day have I perfected your religion for you, completed My favor upon you, and have chosen for you Islam as your religion."** (Sūra 5: Māida, Verse 3).

## 1.1.4 COMPROMISING RELIGIOUS INTEGRITY:

This concept mirrors the views of Jamal al-Din al-Afghani, who advocated for a blending of monotheistic religions. He argued:

> After much research, examination, and reflection, I found that the three monotheistic religions are in complete agreement in both principle and goal. If one of them falls short in some of the absolute commands of goodness, the others complete it! Therefore, it appeared to me that the followers of all three religions should adopt what is common in their essence, origin, and ultimate goal.[47]

---

46  Al-Haddad, (1969 CE). *Madkhal ila al-Hiwar al-Islami al-Masihi*. Al-Matba'a al-Bulisiyya, p. 180 (with modifications).
47  Qasim, Khalid bin Abdullah. *Dialogue with the People of the Book*, p. 123. Available at www.muslim-library.com.

However, such an approach contradicts the Islamic obligation of da'wah, which is explicitly mandated by the Qur'an and Sunnah. Neglecting da'wah to accommodate pluralistic ideals compromises a core responsibility of the Muslim community. Dr. Sayyid Muhammad al-Shahid cautions:

> **66** This is a dangerous matter that no Muslim can accept. The command to call others to Allah ﷻ is clear and explicit in the Qur'an and the Sunnah, and neglecting this call is a violation of one of the most important commandments given to the Muslim Ummah."[48] **99**

Furthermore, what al-Afghani mentions contradicts the Qur'an, which states:

**"This day have I perfected your religion for you completed my favor upon you and have chosen for you Islam as your religion".** (Sūra 5: Māida, verse:3)

And His words:

**"O Apostle! proclaim the (Message) which hath been sent to thee from thy Lord. If thou didst not thou wouldst not have fulfilled and proclaimed His mission:."** (Sūra 5: Māida,67)

And:

**"and follow not their vain desires but beware of them lest they beguile thee from any of that (teaching) which God hath sent down to thee."** (Sūra 5: Māida, verse:49)

## 1.1.5 UNDERMINING THE FINALITY OF ISLAM:

By suggesting that the teachings of Judaism, Christianity, and Islam collectively complete one another, the Abrahamic Project negates the perfection and sufficiency of Islam as declared by Allah in the Qur'an. Such a perspective not only misrepresents Islamic theology but also risks

---

48  Ibid., p. 180.

leading Muslims away from their obligation to preserve and propagate their faith.[49]

## 1.1.6 INVOLVING PARTICIPATION IN THEIR WORSHIP AND RELIGIOUS RITUALS:

One example of this is Pope John Paul II's call for a joint prayer in Assisi on October 27, 1986. He presented himself to the world as the spiritual leader of all religions and as a bearer of the message of peace to all of humanity. His call was met with a number of participants, including Muslims, Jews, Buddhists, and others.

The Pope's invitation had significant results. A global community of believers in God, based on the Christian concept of faith, was established in March 1987. They adopted the slogan: "Believers United," which then expanded to include other calls such as:

- The establishment of a temple for all religions in Sinai.

- A prayer ceremony held in the Cordoba Mosque in 1394 AH, with an invitation extended to celebrate this event as a confirmation of the bonds of brotherhood and love between the followers of Islam and Christianity.

Such events also occurred at various conferences, including one held in Lebanon in 1970, where attendees included three Hindus, four Buddhists, three Muslims, and twenty-eight Christians. There were periods of joint worship led by one of the attendees, with Muslims praying behind idol worshipers, approving of their practices, and even participating in them.

This action is extremely dangerous, as it directly contradicts the verse from the Qur'an:

> 66 **Say: O ye That reject Faith !, I worship not that, Which ye worship, Nor will ye worship, That which I worship. And I will not worship, That which ye have been, Wont**

---

49  Ibid., p. 180.

**to worship, Nor will ye worship, That which I worship. To you be your Way, And to me mine."**

[Sūra 109: Kāfirūn verse:-1- 6] 

The reason for the revelation of this Surah is a well-known incident that parallels this situation. Ibn Ishaq, in his *Sirah*, narrates that Al-Aswad ibn Wa'il Al-Sahmi, a prominent figure among his people, confronted the Prophet ﷺ while he was circumambulating the Ka'bah. He said: "O Muhammad, let us worship what you worship for a year, and you worship what we worship for a year, so we can share in the matter. If what you worship is better than what we worship, we will have gained a share of it." In response to this, Allah ﷻ revealed the verse: *"Say, O disbelievers...".*[50]

Muslim scholars have voiced serious concerns about such actions, highlighting how they undermine the fundamental beliefs of a Muslim. Among these responses is a statement by the late Sheikh Abdulaziz bin Abdullah bin Baz, published in the *Al-Jamia Al-Islamia* magazine, where he clarified:

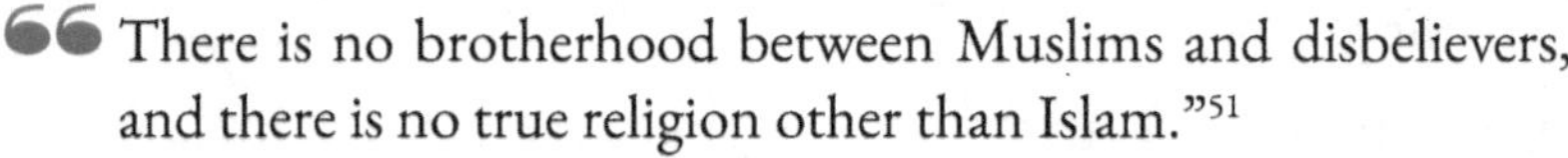

> There is no brotherhood between Muslims and disbelievers, and there is no true religion other than Islam."[51]

This leads to a critical question: How can a Muslim accept an invitation that even Pope Shenouda III, the head of the Coptic Orthodox Church, rejected? He declined to attend a mass held by Pope John Paul II in Cairo, justifying his absence by explaining that the rituals of the Orthodox Church differ from those of the Catholics, despite both sects being part of the Christian faith.

---

50  Ibn Hisham, (1955), *As-Seerah An-Nabawiyyah* (3rd edition), Mustafa al-Babi al-Halabi & Sons Publishing and Printing House (2/10).

51  Al-Shuwa'ir, Muhammad bin Sa'ad. (n.d.). *Wa Lan Tarda 'Anka Al-Yahudu Wa La Al-Nasara. Journal of Islamic Research*, Issue (33), (p. 214).

*Al-Ahram* newspaper, which covered the details of Pope John Paul II's visit to Cairo, reported the incident as follows:

> 66 ... Pope Shenouda III did not attend the mass held by Pope John Paul II in the covered hall at Cairo Stadium. A church official stated that the rituals of this mass differ for the Orthodox compared to the Catholics. While there are shared prayers, there are also many differences in the rites, including this divine liturgy, which is specific to the Catholics. A representative of Pope Shenouda attended instead."[52] 99

Sayyid Qutb comments: "Those who attempt to dilute this clear distinction in the name of tolerance and rapprochement between the Abrahamic faiths misunderstand the true meaning of tolerance. Religion is the final and exclusive truth from God. Tolerance pertains to personal interactions, not to doctrinal beliefs or social systems. They are trying to weaken the firm conviction in a Muslim's heart that God does not accept any religion other than Islam."[53]

What Sayyid Qutb points out about the necessity of maintaining this distinction is crucial. This is the methodology that Muslim preachers should adopt in their dialogues and encounters with people of other faiths. The tolerance prescribed by Islam pertains to personal conduct, but loyalty and mutual support are entirely different concepts that should not be confused with religious beliefs.

---

52  Al-Ahram Newspaper, Saturday, February 21, 2000, p. 2.
53  Qutb, S. (1987). *Fi Zilal al-Qur'an* (13th ed.). Cairo: Dar al-Shorouk.

# 2.0 THE CHALLENGES TO ISLAMIC-JEWISH RECONCILIATION IN ACHIEVING THE ABRAHAMIC DIALOGUE PROJECT

The journey towards reconciliation between Islam and Judaism, especially within the context of the Abrahamic Dialogue Project, is both challenging and complex. This initiative, which aims to foster understanding and cooperation between the three major Abrahamic religions—Judaism, Christianity, and Islam—faces significant obstacles. These hurdles are rooted in a long history of conflict, deep theological differences, and unresolved political issues, particularly the ongoing Israeli-Palestinian conflict. These factors have shaped the relationship between Muslims and Jews over centuries, often leading to mistrust and tension.

At the heart of these challenges are historical memories of violence and oppression. For Muslims, the centuries of conflict with Jewish communities, combined with the trauma of displacement and occupation in Palestine, make it difficult to see the possibility of true reconciliation. On the other side, Jews carry their own painful history of persecution, which feeds their sense of insecurity and the desire to protect their religious and territorial identity.

This section seeks to explore these complex issues and the real barriers that stand in the way of meaningful dialogue. By looking at the historical, theological, and political forces that shape this relationship, this study aims to understand whether genuine reconciliation is possible. Can Muslims and Jews find common ground in the pursuit of peace, or will their past struggles continue to overshadow efforts for cooperation? This question lies at the heart of the Abrahamic Dialogue Project and will be examined in the following discussion.

## 2.1 THE DIFFICULTIES AND OBSTACLES TO RECONCILIATION BETWEEN THE FOLLOWERS OF THE TWO RELIGIONS:

Dialogue aimed at reconciliation plays a crucial role in fostering better relations between Muslims and Jews, particularly when the driving force behind such dialogue is a genuine desire to build a new chapter of mutual respect and understanding. At its core, this dialogue seeks to unite both faiths around the belief that a religion centered on the worship of one God can bring peace to a world that has long suffered from greed, injustice, exploitation, tyranny, and colonization.

However, this noble goal becomes increasingly difficult to achieve when the very followers of these religions, themselves, contribute to the instability and insecurity of the world. When the guiding values of these religious communities reflect greed, injustice, and oppression, rather than the peaceful ideals they claim to uphold, it becomes nearly impossible to convince the world that the true religion of God can offer solutions to these issues.

These deep-rooted problems present significant barriers to dialogue between Muslims and Jews, which ultimately leads to such exchanges becoming irrelevant, and the potential for meaningful discussion fading away.

Moreover, many of the encounters that appear to bring together followers of these religions today are often held alongside Christian communities. The discussions typically focus on broad issues involving all three faiths, often overlooking the deeper doctrinal differences and failing to address the pressing, real-world conflicts and regional tensions that continue to divide them. Even though opportunities exist to resolve these disputes through Abrahamic dialogue, these sessions often miss the mark by not confronting the root issues head-on.

A careful look at history and the current political landscape reveals that the primary obstacles hindering meaningful dialogue between Muslims and Jews are:

## 2.1.1 THE ONGOING JEWISH WARS:

While the Crusades inflicted severe pain upon Muslims and brought them to the brink of devastation, the continuous Jewish attacks and wars on Arab lands in general—and particularly on the Holy Land— have likewise caused immense suffering to Muslims wherever they have settled. These wars have eroded the trust Muslims once had in the prospect of dialogue with Jews and those who support them or follow their lead. The parallel between the Crusades and the Jewish wars is striking for several reasons:

1. **Europe's Role:** Europe played a central role in both the Crusades and the Jewish wars. Today, the United States has largely replaced Europe in supporting the Zionist entity.[54]

2. **Targets Beyond Palestine:** Both the Crusades and the Jewish wars have targeted the broader Arab and Islamic world, not just the land of Palestine. The Crusader campaigns established states and kingdoms, while the Jewish wars have resulted in the occupation of lands in Lebanon, Syria, and Egypt. Furthermore, Israel now seeks to dominate the entire Arab world, guided by the slogan: *"Your land, Israel, extends from the Euphrates to the Nile."*[55]

3. **The Goal of Eradicating Islam:** Both the Crusades and the Jewish wars aimed at eradicating the Islamic presence and replacing it with

---

54 Gazī al-Tawbah, 1998, "Bain al-Ḥamalāt al-Ṣalībīyah wa al-Ḥurūb al-Yahūdīyah – Muqāranah wa Nata'ij," al-Mujtama', al-'Adad 1300, (22-28 Muḥarram 1419 AH - 19-25 May), al-Sanah (29), (p. 28).

55 Ibid., 29

a foreign one—Crusader in the past and Jewish in the present. The goals of both the Crusaders and the Zionists have always extended beyond economic exploitation, seeking instead to establish a permanent and alien presence.[56]

4.  **Timeline of Conflict:** Unlike the Crusades, which began to falter less than fifty years after their inception (in 1144), the Jewish state continues to solidify its power even after nearly eighty years since its establishment.[57]

The primary driving force behind these wars lies in Israel's expansionist ideology and its belief in the concept of the "restored land." Israel Shahak, an Israeli historian, explains that "the main danger posed by Israel, as a Jewish state, to its own people, other Jews, and its neighbors is its ideologically motivated quest for territorial expansion, leading inevitably to a series of wars."[58]

He further comments on their belief in the "restored land," noting: "Israel promotes a discriminatory doctrine among its Jewish citizens regarding the reclamation of land, with the official aim of reducing the number of non-Jews. This ideology is deeply ingrained in Israeli Jewish schools, where students are taught to adopt this mindset."[59]

Looking back at the Crusades, historical studies reveal that Jews played a significant, yet often hidden, role in supporting the Crusaders and pushing for the invasion of the Holy Land. Times Homer explains that the main reason behind Jewish support for these wars was that, unable to return to the Holy Land on their own, the Jews sought to follow the Christians. They used money as a tool, concealing their religious and national motives behind their wealth. Representing the wealthiest commercial centers along the northern Mediterranean

---

56  Ibid., 29

57  Ibid.,29

58  Ishra'il Shahak, 1995, *Al-Tarikh al-Yahudi, al-Diyanah al-Yahudiyah Wata'at Thalathat 'Alam Sanah*, translated by Salih Ali Suwadih, 1st edition, Al-Bayan for Publishing and Distribution, Beirut - Lebanon, September, (p. 18).

59  Ibid.,16

coast, they aided the Crusaders in their mission, which was framed as a Christian cause to open a trade route to the East through Palestine. However, the Jewish cause proved to be far stronger than the Christian cross and more influential than money.[60]

This situation reflects the truth of the Quranic verse: **"Strongest among men in enmity to the believers wilt thou find the Jews and Pagans;"** Sūra 5: Māida, verse: 82).

## 2.1.2 THE PRINCIPLE OF JEWISH SUPERIORITY AND RACIAL DISTINCTION:

According to tradition, Yahweh made a covenant with Abraham, promising that the Jewish people would be set apart and favored above all other nations. This idea is reflected in several verses from the Torah:

> 66 I am the Lord your God, who has separated you from the nations"[61]
>
> "You shall be holy to me, for I am holy. I have separated you from the nations, that you should be mine"[62]
>
> "For you are a holy people to the Lord your God; the Lord has chosen you to be a special people for Himself, above all the nations on the earth. It is not because you are more numerous than other peoples that the Lord has chosen you, but because of His love for you and His faithfulness to the oath He made to your ancestors"[63] 99

In the book of Exodus, it is written: "You have seen what I did to the Egyptians, and how I bore you on eagles' wings and brought you to myself. Now, if you will obey my voice and keep my covenant, you will be a special

---

60 Ahmad Shalaby, 1988, *Comparative Religions: Judaism*, 3rd edition, Al-Nahda Egyptian Library, Cairo (pp. 97, 98) quoted from: James Homer, *The Jews*.
61 (Leviticus 20:24).
62 (Leviticus 20:26).
63 (Deuteronomy 7:6-8).

treasure to me above all people. For all the earth is mine, and you will be to me a kingdom of priests and a holy nation."[64]

These verses emphasize the belief that the Jewish people are uniquely chosen and set apart, with a divine promise to elevate them above others, forming the foundation of their sense of distinction and superiority.[65]

The texts that Jews reference to support their belief as the "chosen people" reflect a deep sense of superiority. They claim that their God, "Yahweh," has specifically set them apart, favoring them over all other nations. In this view, God has driven other peoples out of their lands and given it to the Jewish people.

The Talmud further amplifies this belief in Jewish superiority, suggesting that Jews are a step above the rest of humanity. According to these teachings, non-Jews are seen as servants to the Jewish people, and God has uniquely blessed them with the right to all the earth's blessings. This idea underscores a belief in the separation of the Jewish people and their exclusive entitlement to the wealth and gifts of the world, given only to them by their God.[66]

In the Talmud, Jews are described as a higher form of human being, superior to non-Jews, who are often dehumanized, sometimes even compared to animals. One example from their teachings states that the seed of non-Jews is likened to that of a horse.[67]

Rabbi Menachem once remarked, "O Jews, you are among humanity because your souls come from God's spirit, while the souls of the other nations do not, as their souls come from an impure spirit."[68]

---

64 (Exodus 19:4-6).

65 For further details, see: O'Dea, Janet K., O'Dea, Thomas F., and Adams, Charles J. *Religion and Man: Judaism, Christianity, and Islam.* Harper & Row Publications, 1969, pp. 3-5.

66 Sosa, Ahmad. 1981. *Mufassal al-'Arab wal-Yahud fi al-Tarikh*, 5th ed., Dar al-Rushd, Cairo, pp. 366, 367.

67 Fawour, Asma' Abdulhadi. 1416 AH - 1995 CE. *Filastin wal-Mazari' al-Yahudiya*, 1st ed., Maktabat Dar al-Umma, distributed by Dar al-Nahda al-Islamiyya, Beirut, Lebanon, p. 412. Cited from: *Talmud Urshalim*, p. 94.

68 Ibid., 412

The rabbi Abarbanel once claimed that a non-Jewish woman is like an animal, and that God created the foreigner in human form solely to serve the Jews, for whom the world was made. He argued that it would be improper for a prince to be served by an animal that shares his own form, insisting that this would be against all decency and humanity.[69]

The researcher Arthur Hertzberg further explains that the belief in Jews as God's chosen people originates from the event at Sinai, where God revealed Himself to Moses and the Israelites. According to Hertzberg, this was more than a revelation—it was a "marriage" between God and Israel, formalized by a contract, with the heavens and the earth as witnesses.

He literally stated,

> There are a number of examples in Jewish literature of "A marriage contract" between God and Israel with heaven and earth as witnesses":[70]

In addition, some Jews refer to specific verses from the Qur'an that seem to support their claim to the land of Palestine. One such verse is: **"O children of Israel! call to mind the (special) favor which I bestowed upon You and that I preferred you to all others (for My message)."** (Sūra 2: Baqara, verse:47).

Another verse they cite is: "We **did indeed aforetime Give the Book to Moses : Be not then in doubt of its reaching (thee) : And We made it A guide to the Children Of Israel." "And We appointed, from among Them, Leaders, giving guidance Under Our command, so long As they persevered with patience And continued to have faith In Our Signs"**. (Sūra 32: Sajda, verses,23-24).

While these verses acknowledge the favor bestowed upon the Children of Israel, and confirm their elevated status, the application

---

69  Ibid., 412

70  Shalabi, Ahmad. *Al-Yahudiya* (p. 219), quoted in: Hertzberg, Arthur. *Judaism*, p. 199.

of these verses to justify a claim over the land of Palestine is, in fact, a misinterpretation for the following reasons:

These verses, along with others, acknowledge the Children of Israel and emphasize their preference over the other nations, which is a widely accepted truth. However, applying these verses in this context is not entirely accurate for the following reasons:

1. This preference was granted during their obedience to God and their willingness to endure suffering for His sake.

2. According to most scholars, the verses refer to a specific time, not an eternal condition. They were relevant only during the period when the Israelites responded to God's command, particularly during the time of Moses, peace be upon him, and do not imply an everlasting privilege.

3. The Israelites only remained faithful to this favor for a brief period before they began to deviate during the life of Moses.[71]

Imam Al-Razi offers an explanation: "If someone argues that their preference over the worlds means they are superior to the nation of Muhammad ﷺ this is incorrect. The preference mentioned in the Qur'an was for the people of their time. Those who were not yet born and the Muslim nation, which did not exist back then, were not considered part of the 'worlds' at that time. Therefore, it doesn't necessarily mean that the Israelites were superior to the Muslim nation. This also helps explain verses like: "**R**emember Moses said to his people: "**O my people! call in remembrance the favor of God unto you when He produced prophets among you made you kings and gave you what He had not given to any other among the peoples**". (Sūra 5: Māida, verse:20) and "**And We chose them aforetime Above the nations, knowingly,**" Sūra 44: Dukhān, verse:32)."[72]

---

71 Falistīn wa al-Mazāri' al-Yahūdīyah (p. 393).

72 Al-Rāzī, Muḥammad Fakhr al-Dīn bin Ḍiyā' al-Dīn bin 'Umar. (1995). *Tafsīr Fakhr al-Rāzī al-Mashhūr bi-Tafsīr al-Kabīr wa Mafātīḥ al-Ghayb*, Lebanon, Beirut: Dār al-Fikr li-l-Ṭibā'ah wa al-Nashr (1/355).

These points are further supported by verses from the Qur'an that show their preference was specific to a certain time. Over time, the Israelites earned reproach, curse, and dispersion due to their disobedience, rebellion against their messengers, and killing of prophets.

Allah ﷻ says: "**They were covered with humiliation and misery; they drew on themselves the wrath of God. This because they went on rejecting the signs of God and slaying His messengers without just cause. This because They rebelled and went on transgressing**" (Sūra 2: Baqara, verse:61).

He ﷻ also says: "**Shame is pitched over them (like a tent) wherever they are found except when under a covenant (of protection) from God and from men; they draw on themselves wrath from God and pitched over them is (the tent of) destitution. This because they rejected the signs of God and slew the prophets in defiance of right; this because they rebelled and transgressed beyond bounds.**" (Sūra 3: Āl-i-'Imrān, verse:112).

## 2.1.3 THE JEWISH-ZIONIST CONNECTION: A COMPLEX RELATIONSHIP

While Judaism is a divine religion, and Zionism is a political, racist, and ideological movement aimed at establishing a Jewish state in Palestine, the undeniable truth—confirmed by events and supported by evidence—is that they are inseparable twins, forming an indivisible entity. Zionism is Judaism, and Judaism is Zionism!

The relationship between Judaism and Zionism has not been without internal differences. Religious Jews, for example, often believe that the establishment of a Jewish state must come through divine intervention, while Zionists focus on achieving this goal through human effort. Yet, both groups share a vision of a Jewish homeland, making their differences more about timing and method than about the ultimate goal.

As stated, "Every Jew on earth awaits the establishment of the State of Israel. The difference, if any, lies only in the specifics: religious Jews anticipate the establishment of the State of Israel by a prince descended from David, while Zionists desire its establishment by any means."[73]

Joseph L. Blau observes, "The Zionist movement was not entirely unified—either in purpose or in trajectory—except in its shared desire to establish a homeland for the Jews."[74]

This ultimate Zionist goal in Palestine has been deeply ingrained in the minds of people worldwide. The Jewish community has strived to embed this notion universally to ensure the success of their plan to establish the State of Israel and subsequently work towards the domination they seek.

To accomplish this, Zionists have sought to create a national identity rooted in the Jewish religion, imposing this identity upon Jews worldwide to derive their strength and exert global influence. Consequently, Jews have become wholly aligned with Zionism, to the extent that Jewish thought and imagination have become exclusively Zionist. The unity in purpose, trajectory, vision, and ideology has made separating Zionism from Judaism virtually impossible.

Joseph L. Blau also remarks, "'Zionism captured the imagination of the Jewish masses. It became, for the twentieth century, the vital issue in Jewish life.."[75]

At its core, Zionism was a movement driven by a desire to establish a homeland for the Jewish people. According to Blau, even though there were differences within the movement regarding how to achieve this goal, the shared dream of creating a Jewish state united its followers. For many, this dream was not just political but deeply tied to their sense of identity and faith.

---

73  Marsafi, Saad. Al-Rasul ﷺ Wajhan li-Wajh (The Prophet ﷺ Face to Face). Maktabat al-Manar al-Islamiyyah, First ed., Hawalli, Kuwait, 1413 AH-1992 CE, p. 47.

74  Blau, Joseph L. Modern Varieties of Judaism. Lectures on the History of Religions, sponsored by the American Council of Learned Societies, New Series, no. 8, Columbia University Press, 1964. Reprint 1966, p. 145.

75  Ibi., p. 145

The words of Zionist leaders further demonstrate this inseparable connection. Chaim Weizmann stated: "Our Judaism and our Zionism are inseparable and intertwined. Destroying Zionism would entail destroying Judaism itself."[76]

Some have described Zionism as an expression of Jewish belief, culture, and history in theory, paired with the practical effort of migrating to Palestine to build a nation. As Solomon Schechter observed: "Wherever Zionists are active, Judaism thrives and flourishes."[77]

The founder of the Zionist movement, Theodor Herzl, clarified the connection between Judaism and Zionism in 1897 (1315 AH) by stating: "The return to Zion must be preceded by a return to Judaism."[78]

Dr. Yusuf al-Qaradawi observed: "Since Zionism is a political movement rooted in religion, countering it must also employ religion."[79]

Dr. Saad al-Marsafi summarized: "Judaism is Zionism, and every Jew is a Zionist, whether religious or secular. Evidence of this is found in the actions of Jewish rabbis who worked for the establishment of the State of Israel, celebrated its foundation, and supported it alongside their religious followers."[80]

The bond between Judaism and Zionism, shaped by history, ideology, and collective aspiration, remains a topic of intense debate, reflecting both shared visions and complex realities.

---

76 Susa, Ahmad. Mufassal al-'Arab wa al-Yahud fi al-Tarikh (A Detailed Account of Arabs and Jews in History). p. 693.

77 Rushdi, Omar. Al-Sihyuniyyah wa Rabibatuhā Isra'il (Zionism and Its Offspring, Israel). 2nd ed., Cairo, Egypt, 1385 AH-1965 CE, p. 45.

78 Qaradawi, Yusuf. Dars al-Nakbah al-Thaniyah: Limādhā Inhazamnā... Wa Kayfa Nantasir (The Lesson of the Second Nakba: Why We Were Defeated... and How We Can Triumph). 2nd ed., Beirut, Dar al-Fikr, 1391 AH-1971 CE, p. 77.

79 Ibid., p. 77

80 Ibid., p. 88

## 2.2 THE RESULT OF THESE OBSTACLES AND THE PROPOSED SOLUTIONS:

There is no doubt that the aforementioned obstacles prevent the realization of the goals of the Abrahamic project. It is impossible to create a climate of dialogue and rapprochement under its umbrella, given the prevailing conditions that stem from the devastating battles, various wars, and ongoing conspiracies that have planted mutual distrust and suspicion.

Professor Ismail Raja al-Faruqi points out the result of these negative phenomena, saying:

> Muslim-Jewish dialogue is still non existent. It has absolutely nothing to show for its self: No precedent, not even a hypothetical agenda The Creation of the state of Israel and the continuous hostility this had engendered between Jewry and the Muslim world prevented any religious dialogue from taking place."[81]

It is as though we are seeing history repeating itself today, where Professor Ismail Raja could be witnessing what Muslims are currently facing in the land of Jihad, the massacres at the hands of the Jews, who have opposed the dialogue table on multiple occasions to stop the bloodshed of Muslims in Gaza.

It seems that the path toward a fruitful dialogue between Muslims and Jews can only be achieved through the following steps:

- **Firstly**: Zionism must declare itself as a racist and ideological movement, foreign to Palestine and the Middle East. It cannot be connected to Judaism, which is a heavenly religion.

- **Secondly**: Dialogue between Jews and Muslims must be based on the Abrahamic faith that they share, where disputes and conflicts

---

81  Al-Faruqi, Ismail Raja. Trialogue of the Abrahamic Faiths. International Institute of Islamic Thought, Herndon, Virginia, USA, 1991. Forward, p. 3.

are resolved in light of the Abrahamic religious vision of these differences.

- **Thirdly**: The Islamic view of Jews should be a faith-based perspective, assessing their individuals as either believers or non-believers, not based on ethnicity or nationality, as Jews view their ancestors through a nationalistic lens, often leading them to interact with each other in a racial, nationalistic manner.[82]

- **Fourthly**: Jews must liberate themselves from the ideology of tension, chaos, crime, and division, as well as the ongoing animosity towards Muslims.

- **Fifthly**: The core issue, above all else, is the liberation of Palestine and the return of Palestinians, so that a Palestinian state can be established where Muslims, Christians, and Jews coexist peacefully.

These points, among others, may offer solutions to the problems at hand and create a climate for religious dialogue that could resolve disputes, diminish enmities, and foster purity and love in the hearts.

Dr. Emil Habibi states: "... The truth is that our problem is not with the relations between the three religions, but with the policies... However, the three religions should be absolved from being the cause of the issues between us."[83]

---

82  Al-Khalidi, Salah. Haqa'iq Qur'aniyah Hawla al-Qadiyah al-Filastiniyah. 2nd ed., Manshurat Filastin al-Muslimah, 1995, pp. 79-80.

83  Habibi, Emil. Bahuth al-Nadwah al-'Alamiyyah Hawl al-Quds wa Turathaha al-Thaqafi fi Itar al-Hiwar al-Islami al-Masihi. Rabat, 3-5 Jumada al-Awwal 1414 AH - 29-21 October 1993 CE. Keynote speech titled: "Tassawur Mustaqbali lil-'Alaqat al-Thaqafiyyah Bayn al-Diyanat al-Thalath fi al-Madinah al-Muqaddasah," by Dr. Emil Habibi. Manshurat al-Munazzamah al-Islamiyyah li-l-Tarbiyyah wa-l-'Ulum al-Thaqafiyyah (ISESCO), 1995, p. 714.

# 3.0 CHALLENGES TO ISLAMIC-CHRISTIAN CONVERGENCE IN REALIZING THE ABRAHAMIC DIALOGUE PROJECT

## 3.1 INTRODUCTION TO ISLAMIC-CHRISTIAN RELATIONS:

The contemporary world is teeming with a multitude of religions and sects, which no reasonable person can ignore. Among these, certain religions demonstrate a closer affinity to Islam than others—an undeniable truth highlighted in multiple Quranic verses. For instance, Allah ﷻ states:

> Strongest among men in enmity to the believers wilt thou find the Jews and Pagans; and nearest among them in love to the believers wilt thou find those who say: "We are Christians:" because amongst these are men devoted to learning and men who have renounced the world and they are not arrogant. And when they listen to the revelation received by the Apostle thou wilt see their eyes overflowing with tears for they recognize the truth: they pray: "Our Lord! we believe; write us down among the witnesses. "What cause can we have not to believe in God and the truth which has come to us seeing that

**we long for our Lord to admit us to the company of the righteous?"**

(Sūra 5: Māida,Verses :82–85) 99

---

Joseph van Ess comments on this dynamic: "Islam's stance towards Christianity differs significantly from its stance towards Judaism. Christianity is closer to Islam than Judaism, and the disagreement between Islam and Christianity has often been theological, interspersed with instances of praise for certain Christians. By contrast, the animosity between Islam and Judaism has been more pronounced, with Islam adopting a harsher stance towards Jews than Christians. After Islam's triumph in the Arabian Peninsula, Christians and Jews were allowed to maintain their faith as 'People of the Book,' in contrast to idolaters. Even today, in many Muslim countries, Christian clergy enjoy considerable respect from Muslims."[84]

Due to this profound and historical relationship, as well as the tangible and intangible connections between the two faiths, various dialogue meetings have taken place. These gatherings have brought adherents of both religions together to discuss a wide range of issues, significantly contributing to strengthening and developing their relations. Over time, this dialogue has evolved into a platform for mutual understanding and collaboration on shared principles, aiming to serve humanity's welfare and mitigate potential harms.

## 3.2 CHALLENGES AND OBSTACLES TO ISLAMIC-CHRISTIAN CONVERGENCE WITHIN THE FRAMEWORK OF THE ABRAHAMIC PROJECT

Dialogues between followers of Islam and Christianity continue to face significant barriers of mutual mistrust and skepticism. These

---

84  Al-Shāhid, Muḥammad. (1994 CE). Ḥiwār al-Masīḥiyya wa-al-Islām fī al-Tawḥīd wa-al-Nubuwwa wa-al-Qur'ān: Dirāsa Taḥlīliyya Naqdiyya li-Ārā' Hāns Kung wa-Jūzif Fān I*. Al-Mu'assasa al-Jāmi'iyya lil-Dirāsāt wa-al-Nashr wa-al-Tawzī', Bayrūt, al-Ṭab'a al-Ūlā, 1414 AH–1994 CE, (p. 59).

sentiments are deeply rooted in the lingering negative impacts of historical conflicts and wars, coupled with doctrinal differences stemming from what Muslims perceive as the distortion of Christian sacred texts.

Given these complexities, the challenges[85] hindering Islamic-Christian rapprochement can be categorized as follows:

## 3.2.1 THE HISTORICAL AND CONTEMPORARY POLITICAL-RELIGIOUS ENTANGLEMENTS BETWEEN EAST AND WEST:

### - Defining "East" and "West"

In this context, "the West" refers to the predominantly Christian societies historically concentrated in Europe, which later shifted political and cultural prominence to the America. Meanwhile, "the East" represents predominantly Islamic societies rooted in the Arab world, home to significant religious sanctities, even as demographic weight has shifted towards the heart of Asia.[86]

This delineation captures the historical and cultural duality that continues to shape interactions between the two civilizations, where politics and religion have been deeply interwoven, often complicating efforts toward reconciliation and dialogue.

## 3.3 POLITICAL AND RELIGIOUS ENTANGLEMENTS IN THE PAST:

Historically, the Christian West has engaged in aggression against the East, often invading its lands, desecrating its sanctities, violating its people, and plundering its resources and cultural wealth. This hostility stemmed largely from the West's desire to exploit the East's abundant agricultural and commercial riches, its philosophical and civilizational

---

85　Ṣiddīqī, ʿAṭāʾullāh. (Sep. 1996). "Christian-Muslim Dialogue: Problems and Challenges," Encounters: Journal of Intercultural Perspectives, Vol. 2, No. 2, pp. 122–133.

86　Al-Ḥūrānī, ʿAbdullāh. (Ṣafar 1416 AH, Issue 185, Year 14). Daʿwat al-Ḥaqq: al-Ḥiwār al-Nāfiʿ bayna Aṣḥāb al-Sharāʾiʿ, (p. 45).

heritage, and, in more recent times, its vast reserves of mineral, petroleum, and strategic resources.

This animosity and political resentment are not recent phenomena. Their roots can be traced back to the era of the Islamic conquests, when Muslims took control of territories that had been part of the Byzantine Empire. These events fostered long-standing fears and hostility, especially as Islam emerged as a formidable presence perceived as a threat to the Christian world. Religious leaders, monarchs, and feudal elites in the West were among those who benefited from and perpetuated this enmity.[87]

The Crusades are a glaring manifestation of these deep-seated hostilities, which were exacerbated by the retreat of Europeans from Eastern lands. Later, the so-called Age of Exploration was not merely an era of discovering unknown territories but a calculated effort to reconnect with and exploit the riches of the East. These "discoveries" were of regions with established systems and laws, not uncharted wilderness.

Prince Henry the Navigator of Portugal, a key figure in these exploratory ventures, was not just a maritime pioneer. He had previously participated in campaigns against Muslims alongside his father, using these voyages as a means to encircle and dominate the Islamic world. The discovery of the Americas, often romanticized as a quest for new lands, was in fact motivated by the desire to reach India, then under Islamic rule. This so-called exploration was the first step in a broader strategy of dominating Islamic territories.

Following Portugal and Spain, England and France took up the mantle, with other European powers such as the Netherlands also joining the fray. These nations, under the banners of colonialism and expansion, intensified their antagonism toward Islamic lands, asserting control over them in a pursuit driven by both economic interests and deep-seated political animosities.[88]

---

87  Ibid., P. 49

88  Al-Nimr, ʿAbd al-Munʿim. (1982 CE). Al-Islām wa-al-Gharb Wajhan li-Wajh,

To ensure historical accuracy and religious impartiality, we can refer to the *Arab Encyclopedia*, a notable work significantly shaped by contributions from Eastern Christians. The encyclopedia states:

> The immediate impetus for the Crusades was the sermon delivered by Pope Urban II at the Council of Clermont in 1095 CE. In his address, he urged the Christian world to embark on a war to liberate the Holy Sepulchre from the Muslims. He promised those who joined the campaign a plenary indulgence for their sins and offered general assurances that their homes would be protected during their absence. The Crusaders took their name from the crosses distributed to them during the meeting. While religious motives were undoubtedly strong, other worldly incentives also played a role. Nobles sought spoils and the establishment of new principalities, the Normans pursued territorial expansion at the expense of both Byzantines and Muslims, and Italian city-states aimed to expand their trade networks in the East. All of these were driven, to some extent, by the allure of adventure and exploration."[89]

These factors fueled what became the first major global conflict, lasting nearly two centuries, and mobilized nearly all European nations against Arabs, Turks, and others. Tragically, these Crusades went far beyond a mission to reclaim the Holy Sepulchre.

Leduc de Castris, a member of the French Academy, citing Robert Moine, recounts Pope Urban II's rallying call for the Crusades. The pope described the Islamic world in the following terms:

---

Al-Mu'assasa al-Jāmi'iyya lil-Dirāsāt, Bayrūt, (p. 47).
89  al-Ḥiwār al-Nāfi' bayna Aṣḥāb al-Sharā'i', (p. 55).

> 66 A cursed nation, a people entirely alien to God, a community that has neither turned its heart nor its soul toward Him. This nation has seized lands that rightly belong to Christians."[90] 99

Addressing his audience and Christians at large, Pope Urban II further declared:

> 66 Do not let concerns about your estates or family affairs deter you from this mission. The land you inhabit is confined by seas and mountains, leaving your people in overcrowded and limited spaces. Its resources are meager, offering little sustenance even to those who cultivate it. This scarcity has caused division and conflict among you."[91] 99

He continued by glorifying the Christians present, urging them:

---

90 Al-'Ayyāshūbī, Muḥammad. (Feb. 1976 CE, Ṣafar 1396 AH). "How to Work on Removing Incorrect Prejudices and the Lack of Trust That Still Divide Us," Research and Documents of the Islamic-Christian Dialogue Seminar, Tripoli, (2-6), Prepared and Published by the External Communications Office of the General People's Congress, the Great Socialist People's Libyan Arab Jamahiriya, 1390 AH–1981 CE, (pp. 350, 351) Quoted from: La Conquête de la Terre Sainte Par les Croisés, Éditions Albin Michel, Paris, Al-'Ayyāshūbī, Muḥammad. (Feb. 1976 CE, Ṣafar 1396 AH). "How to Work on Removing Incorrect Prejudices and the Lack of Trust That Still Divide Us," Research and Documents of the Islamic-Christian Dialogue Seminar, Tripoli, (2-6), Prepared and Published by the External Communications Office of the General People's Congress, the Great Socialist People's Libyan Arab Jamahiriya, 1390 AH–1981 CE, (pp. 350, 351) Quoted from: La Conquête de la Terre Sainte Par les Croisés, Éditions Albin Michel, Paris, p. 195.

91 Ibid., P.195

> 66 Set forth toward the path of the Holy Sepulchre. Wrest that land from the hands of these profane peoples, and subject it to your dominion."[92] 99

This rhetoric, steeped in religious zeal and laced with worldly incentives, illustrates the complex motivations behind the Crusades and their devastating impact on both the East and West.

From this famous call by Pope Urban II, it can be inferred that the desire to reclaim the tomb of Christ was not the sole justification for the fierce attack on the Islamic world. Rather, there were economic and human factors that, alongside spiritual motives, helped to justify the outbreak of violence that heralded the colonial era. Christians, in addition to fulfilling their religious duty, were urged to set aside their internal divisions caused by a lack of wealth and to "subjugate" Islamic lands under their control. As a result, Western lords and states continued to seize Islamic territories, turning them into feudal fiefs and dominions.[93]

Professor Perroy, an honorary professor at the Sorbonne, wrote: "In reality, there is no evidence that prior to Urban II, the papacy cared about the fate of the Holy Land or the protection of its visitors from the Muslims."[94]

Gerard Walter, who wrote the introduction to De Castris' book *The Conquest of the Holy Land by the Italian Capitalists*, mentioned that warships stationed in Italian ports supported the Crusader armies, bringing with them troops funded by businessmen from Genoa, Pisa, and Venice. He added, "From that time, the merchants of Venice became the masters of the Syrian coast."[95]

---

92  Ibid., P.195
93  Ibid., P. 351
94  Ibid., P. 351
95  Ibid., P. 351

After presenting these historical facts and documents during the seminar, Muhammad al-ʿAyyāshūbī concluded: "The Crusades were, in reality, an arbitrary transfer of wealth. In this way, the economic life of the Mediterranean evolved. As colonialism expanded and colonial armies carried out their conquests, Europe, Africa, and Asia were drastically altered, changing the course of history. During the Industrial Revolution, this led to a disruption of the global economy, creating new relationships founded on conquest and control. The consequences of these relationships are still felt in our world today. The world has been divided into two parts: one living in wealth and technology, the other in hunger and illiteracy. How can we reconcile all of this? Are certain nations doomed to bear the burden of political and economic injustices from the powerful forever?"[96]

During the Crusades, which lasted for nearly two centuries in the Levant and even attempted to extend into the holy cities of Mecca and Medina, the Christian crusaders were resolute in their mission to assert their faith as the ultimate truth. They sought to forcibly convert people and eliminate those who opposed their beliefs.

The historian Will Durant, in his encyclopedic work translated into Arabic, quotes Father Raymond of Aguilers, who witnessed one such massacre. Father Raymond described:

> We saw amazing sights: the heads of a great number of Muslims were severed, others were killed by arrows, and some were forced to leap from the towers. Others were tortured for days before being burned alive. The streets were filled with piles of heads, hands, and feet. Wherever one rode on horseback, it was over the bodies of men and horses."[97]

Another eyewitness recounted:

---

96  Ibid., P. 353
97  Will Dūrānt, (d. t.) Qiṣṣat al-Ḥaḍārah al-Sharq al-Adnā, Tarjamah Muḥammad Badr, al-Hay'ah al-Miṣrīyah al-ʿĀmmah lil-Kitāb (4/25).

> ❝ Women were slaughtered with swords and lances, infants were torn from their mothers' breasts by their legs and thrown from bridges, or their heads were smashed with clubs. Seventy thousand Muslims who remained in the city were massacred."[98] ❞

The Church continued its campaign to expel Muslims from Andalusia, compelling those who remained to convert to Christianity. Converts were monitored in their homes to ensure they showed no outward signs of Islamic affiliation, whether in clothing, diet, hygiene practices, or names. Practices like worship and reading the Qur'an were strictly prohibited, and severe punishments were inflicted on those who were caught observing Islamic traditions, avoiding church attendance, or speaking or writing in Arabic.[99]

The crusaders' actions during this period represented the height of fanaticism. For two centuries, starting in 490 AH, relentless campaigns were launched against Islamic lands. When a city or village was conquered, its inhabitants were often subjected to extreme brutality. Neither peaceful Muslims nor neutral Jews were spared.

In his *History of the Crusades*, Michaud, as quoted by Sheikh Muhammad al-Ghazali, highlighted the stark contrast between Muslim and Christian conquests of Jerusalem:

"When Umar ibn al-Khattab took Jerusalem, no harm befell the Christians. However, when the Christians regained it, they slaughtered Muslims and burned Jews alive."[100]

Ibn Kathir, recounting the events of 492 AH, noted that the Crusaders killed 60,000 Muslims upon capturing Jerusalem. He further cited Ibn al-Jawzi, stating:

---

98  Ibid.,25-26
99  Ibid.,P.26
100  al-Ghazālī, Muḥammad, (1990 CE). al-Taʿaṣṣub wa-al-Tasāmuḥ bayna al-Masīḥīyah wa-al-Islām, Maṭbaʿat Iḥsān, Kuwait, (pp. 196–199).

"They seized 42 silver lamps and 23 golden lamps from around the Dome of the Rock."[101]

These accounts underscore the ferocity and destruction wrought by the Crusaders, shaping a legacy of violence and religious animosity during this turbulent era.

When Christians gained control of Andalusia, they systematically stripped Muslims of basic freedoms through public royal decrees. Among these were:

1. **Book Burning (1501 CE):** A royal decree mandated the burning of all religious books in the possession of Muslim Moriscos.[102]

2. **Conversion of Mosques (1533 CE):** All mosques were repurposed as churches.[103]

3. **Burial Prohibition (1524 CE):** Muslims were forbidden from burying their dead in their farmlands or having dedicated cemeteries, forcing them to bury their dead in Christian churches or monasteries.[104]

4. **Forced Conversion (September 13, 1525 CE):** The persecution reached its peak with a royal edict imposing mandatory conversion to Christianity. Islamic practices such as circumcision and the use of Islamic names were outlawed. Muslims often resorted to giving their children two names—one secret Islamic name and another public Christian one. Additionally, they were prohibited from performing

---

101 Ibn Kathīr, Abū al-Fidā' al-Ḥāfiẓ Ibn Kathīr al-Dimashqī. al-Bidāyah wa-al-Nihāyah, taḥqīq Dr. Aḥmad Abū Milḥam, Dr. ʿAlī Najīb ʿAṭwī, al-Ustadh Fuʾād al-Sayyid, wa-al-Ustadh Nāṣir al-Dīn, Lebanon: Beirut: Dār al-Kutub al-ʿIlmīyah, (12/156).

102 Hurtz, Antōnyū Duminyqīr al-Faransī, Barnārd Btthnt. (1988). *Tārīkh Muslimī al-Andalus "al-Mūrīskiyīn" Ḥayāt wa-Maʾsāt Aqlīyah*, translated by: ʿAbd al-ʿĀl Ṣāliḥ, introduced and supplemented by: Muḥammad Muḥī al-Dīn al-Aṣfar. Qaṭar: Dār al-Ishrāq, al-Ṭabʿah al-Ūlā, 1408 AH–1988 CE, (p. 125).

103 Ibid.,59

104 Ibid.,P.128

Islamic ritual slaughter and were required to employ Christian butchers for their meat.[105]

To enforce these decrees, the infamous **Inquisition Courts** were established. These courts played a central role in rooting out Islamic practices through surveillance, forced compliance, confiscation of property, and harsh taxes. Violence and fear were their hallmark. There was no tolerance for any Islamic rituals; the explicit aim was the complete eradication of Islam from Andalusia.[106]

This historical backdrop of persecution has engendered suspicion and even pessimism about calls for interfaith dialogue, particularly when initiated by Christian institutions such as the Catholic or Protestant Churches. Many Muslims perceive these overtures as veiled attempts at proselytization rather than genuine efforts for understanding or collaboration.

Such doubts are reinforced by statements from prominent Christian missionaries acknowledging the failure of traditional methods of proselytization and advocating for more subtle, effective strategies. This includes framing dialogue as a means to foster unity among religions, promote peace, or combat atheism—objectives publicly declared by organizers of these events. This perceived hidden agenda fuels mistrust, as many see dialogue as merely a "new guise" for the same proselytizing mission[107].

## 3.4 POLITICAL ENTANGLEMENT IN THE PRESENT:

If we consider this as a distorted image of the past history, shaped in the minds of Muslims (as argued by those who reject these facts), a false image that tarnishes the reputation of the West, and that Muslims should forget and rewrite history to reach a new advanced stage free from past grudges and hostilities, then the current Western political situation that

---

105  Ibid.,P.115

106  Ibid.,P.64

107  al-Duktūr al-Sayyid Muḥammad al-Shāhid. Ḥiwār al-Masīḥīyah wa-al-Islām fī al-Tawḥīd wa-al-Nubuwwah wa-al-Qur'ān, (p. 5).

the entire world is witnessing today serves as blatant evidence, affirming the credibility of the past. The objectives of those bloody wars are still materializing in reality, with the West striving to achieve its political interests and ambitions. The events of the present phase are merely a continuation of the past era; a fact that threatens the future of dialogue and rapprochement between Muslims and the West, creating a major obstacle in the relationship and cooperation between the two sides in various areas such as political, economic, intellectual, and social matters, among others. Roger Garaudy asserts,

> Western civilization's rise and progress have been linked to its brutal, destructive approach toward weak nations and its plundering of their resources through methods that reflect cunning, deceit, and a lack of noble values. The examples of the East India Company in India, the Dutch company in Indonesia, the African slave trade to America, the extermination of Native Americans, the persecution of indigenous Australians, the Opium Wars in China, and the exploitation of gold mines in South Africa and Guinea, are just a few of many such examples."[108]

Huntington notes,

> After World War 11, the West, in turn, began to retreat; the colonial empires disappeared; first Arab nationalism and then Islamic fundamentalism manifested themselves; the West became heavily dependent on the Persian Gulf countries for its energy; the oil-rich Muslim countries became moneyrich and, when they wished to, weapons-rich. Several wars occurred between Arabs and Israel (created by the West). France fought a bloody and ruthless war in Algeria for most of the 1950; British and French forces invaded Egypt in 1956;

---

108  Jaroudi, Roger. (1986 CE). *Hewar al-Hadharat*, Muncharat Awidat, Beirut, 3rd edition, (pp. 37-93), in which he provides an accurate account of the actions of colonizers in Asia and Africa.

American forces went into Lebanon in 1958; subsequently American forces returned to Lebanon, attacked Libya, and engaged in various military encounters with Iran; Arab and Islamic terrorists, supported by at least three Middle Eastern governments, employed the weapon of the weak and bombed Western planes and installations and seized Western hostages. This warfare between Arabs and the West culminated in 1990, when the United States sent a massive army to the Persian Gulf to defend some Arab countries against aggression by another. In its aftermath NATO planning is increasingly directed to potential threats and instability along its "southern tier.".[109]

He also explains that the West exploits international institutions, military power, and economic resources to manage the world in ways that preserve its dominance, protect Western interests, and promote the political and economic values of the West.

Furthermore, he points out that the decisions made in the United Nations Security Council or the International Monetary Fund, which reflect Western interests, are presented to the world as representing the will of the international community. The term "international community" has evolved into an encompassing term, replacing "the free world," to lend global legitimacy to actions that reflect the interests of the United States and other Western powers. Through the International Monetary Fund and other economic institutions, the West advances its economic interests and imposes economic policies on other countries that it considers appropriate.

He also notes that in the post-Cold War world, the primary goal of arms control is to prevent non-Western societies from developing

---

109 Huntington, Samuel P. (1995 CE). *Islam and the West: The Clash of Civilizations*, translated by Muhammad Shar Shar, Madbouly Library, Beirut, 3rd edition, (p. 23). Or **Huntington, Samuel P.** "The Clash of Civilizations?" *Foreign Affairs*, Summer 1993, vol. 72, no. 3, pp. 22-49. *GRIP*, 1993, www.grip. org/wp-content/uploads/2003/05/THE-CLASH-OF-CIVILIZATIONS_1993_ Huntington.pdf.

military capabilities that could pose a threat to Western interests. The West seeks to achieve this goal through international agreements, economic pressure, and restrictions on the transfer of arms and weapon technologies.

As a result of these Western actions against Muslims, reactions emerged from Islamic groups that awakened the entire Islamic world, warning of dire consequences. They called for preparations to defend Islamic lands from the threat of Western domination spreading throughout the Islamic East. This threat would reveal its consequences if the period of Western control were prolonged and solidified in the East. The Islamists began to realize the bleak future and the significant misfortune that would befall Islam and Muslims if the situation in the Islamic East persisted as it was.[110]

Among the Islamic thinkers who raised awareness and spread intellectual teachings was Jamal al-Din al-Afghani, who stated: "The Christian world, despite the differences in its nations and peoples, whether in terms of race or nationality, is an enemy that stands opposed to the East in general and to Islam in particular. All Christian nations are united in their efforts to bring down the Islamic kingdoms as much as they can."[111]

He further emphasized that "the Crusading spirit has remained dormant in the hearts of Christians, like fire hidden beneath the ashes, and the spirit of intolerance has remained alive and agitated within them to this day, just as it was in the heart of Peter the Hermit. Christianity has always carried within it an element of fanaticism, deeply ingrained in its very essence, and it continues to view Islam with hostility, hatred, and contempt for religious diversity. The reality of this situation and its outcome are evident in many serious matters and major issues, where international laws and conventions have not treated Muslim nations on an equal footing with Christian nations."[112]

---

110  Ibid., 23-55
111  Quoted from 'an: al-Islām wa al-Ṣirāʿāt al-Dīnīyah, (ṣ. 219).
112  Ibid., P.219

Al-Afghani continued: "Christian nations fabricate excuses for their hatred, attacks, and aggression against Islamic kingdoms, subjecting them to humiliation and coercion, by claiming that these Islamic nations are so degenerate and backward that they are incapable of managing their own affairs. Moreover, these same Christian nations have not ceased to act in this manner, using a myriad of justifications, even resorting to war, force, and violence to crush any movement attempted by Muslims in their own lands for reform and revival."[113]

He concluded: "All Christian nations are united in their animosity towards Islam, with the spirit of this enmity embodied in the covert, hidden efforts of all these nations to utterly crush Islam."[114]

## 3.4.1 THE UNIPOLARITY OF THE CHRISTIAN WEST, ITS SOVEREIGNTY, AND ITS VIEW OF OTHER PEOPLES:

The West has been shaped by its historical legacy, intellectual heritage, and colonialist perspective, which fosters a sense of superiority and arrogance toward other peoples. This view is not based on equality, reciprocity, or mutual exchange, but rather on a unilateral belief that the West possesses a civilization and culture that represents the culmination of all civilizations and cultures. The collapse of the socialist system further reinforced this view, allowing Western dominance to lead the world.

Dr. Ahmed Mohamed Al-Asaal states: "Writings justifying this unipolarity, such as those by Francis Fukuyama, emerged. Fukuyama speaks of the 'end of history,' claiming that the entire world has reached a sort of consensus regarding liberal democracy as a system of governance after the defeat of competing ideologies. Fukuyama argues that both Hegel and Marx saw history reaching its end when humanity achieves a form of society that meets the essential and primary needs of humans. For Hegel, this was liberalism, and for Marx, it was a communist society."[115]

---

113  Ibid., P.219
114  Ibid., P-219
115  Al-Asaal, Ahmed Mohamed. (1416 AH-1996 CE). *Hiwar al-Hadarat: Madkhal ila Ru'ya Islamiyya*, 1st edition, Maktabat Wahba, Cairo, (pp. 46, 47).

This unipolarity is also emphasized by Samuel Huntington in *The Clash of Civilizations*, where he argues that the forthcoming conflict will be a clash between civilizations, in which Western civilization will seek to dismantle those civilizations that continue to preserve their sense of identity and distinctiveness.[116]

This absolute sovereignty, coupled with its dominance in military and political spheres, has generated in the West a complex of arrogance and pride. This attitude forms a significant barrier to any hopeful project of dialogue with the West, despite the varying levels and diverse objectives of such dialogue initiatives.

This reflects the same behavior from the past that has undermined relations between the East and the West for centuries, paving the way for the Crusades, justifying colonization, and violating the sanctity of nations. Even today, this attitude takes on many forms, appearing at times in the name of religion, at other times under the guise of culture, humanity, civilization, or democracy.

The unipolarity enjoyed by the Christian West has fostered arrogance and pride, leading it to urge non-Western nations to adopt Western values, integrate with the West, and accept its institutions. This approach is fundamentally at odds with Islam's worldview, which offers distinct cosmic, civilizational, and humanistic perspectives. Western values, in all their forms, are simply not acceptable to Islamic societies and are also rejected by most non-Western societies.

In future projections for international politics, Kishore asserts that the central axis of future international politics will be the conflict between the West and the rest, with non-Western civilizations responding to Western power and values.[117]

Huntington also points out that the efforts made by the United States and other Western powers to persuade other nations to adopt Western ideas related to democracy and human rights are essentially part

---

116  The Clash of Civilizations, 16
117  Ibid., P.46. Quoted from Mahtbuban, Kishore. The East and the West. pp. 3-13.

of a strategy to promote Western colonial interests and maintain control over non-Western societies. Huntington states that modern democratic governments originated in the West, and when they were established in non-Western societies, they were typically the product of Western colonialism or imposition[118].

He further adds that a scholar who reviewed one hundred comparative studies on values across different societies concluded that the values most important in the West are of much lesser significance in many other parts of the world.[119]

This is entirely natural, as each side has its own belief system, philosophy, and worldview, which align with what it desires and is consistent with the spirit, methods, and principles it upholds.

## 3.4.2 THE CHRISTIAN WEST'S SUPPORT FOR THE ESTABLISHMENT OF THE ZIONIST ENTITY IN THE HEART OF THE ISLAMIC WORLD:

The establishment of the Zionist entity in the heart of the Islamic world, supported by Protestant America to impose its military superiority over the entire Islamic world, does not truly pave the way for Christian-Muslim encounters to advance to a stage of genuine dialogue for peaceful coexistence among people of different faiths or for fostering a psychological readiness or trust.[120]

This is evident in the calls and appeals made by high-ranking Western Christian authorities, which were unjust toward the Islamic nation and often denied its rights in many ways.

Such unjust calls, as pointed out by Dr. Abdulrahman Al-Hourani, are represented in the message sent by Pope Paul VI after the 1967 debacle between the Arabs and the Zionist entity. He suggested designating the

---

118   The Clash of Civilizations,45

119   Ibid., 45, Quoted from Trains, Harry C. "Cross-Cultural Studies of Individualism and Collectivism." The New York Times, 23 Dec. 1990, p. 41. Nebraska Symposium on Motivation, vol. 37, 1989, pp. 41-133.

120   Al-Hiwar al-Nafi' Bayn Ashab al-Shara'i' (p. 80).

first day of 1968 as "World Peace Day," at a time when large parts of the Islamic world were under Israeli occupation, from the eastern Nile Delta to the outskirts of Damascus. Meanwhile, NATO fleets, American forces, and their European bases were providing continuous support, intervention, and intelligence at every moment.[121]

Dr. Abdulrahman Al-Hourani quotes the Pope's message: "The Catholic Church calls upon us to observe 'World Peace Day' according to the religious and ethical expressions of the Christian doctrine. However, it considers it its duty to remind everyone that such a day must be characterized by certain points: The first of these is the necessity of defending peace against the dangers that threaten it—namely, the remnants of selfishness in international relations and the danger of violence, which some societies may allow themselves to indulge in due to despair, as they have not been granted the right to life and human dignity in a recognized and respected manner."[122]

This reflects the Catholic attitude toward Islam, which, in itself, is less extreme and biased than Protestantism, which, since the 16th century, began adopting Zionist dreams and visions and collaborating with them to shape political, economic, and military events.

## 3.4.3 ATTEMPTS OF CRUSADING WESTERN MISSIONARY WORK THROUGH WESTERN COLONIAL INFLUENCE:

This is evident in the activities carried out at the heart of the world and its peripheries, particularly in Africa and parts of the Islamic East. The Christian West itself is more in need of spiritual life, love, and religious peace than the Islamic East.

While missionary work may initially appear as a noble cause, akin to the Islamic call for spreading God's teachings, it has another clear and tangible objective. In reality, the aim is to weaken Muslims and transform them into pliable tools in the hands of the West and global Zionism.[123]

---

121  Ibid., P.82

122  Ibid., P. 82-83

123  Furukh, Omar, & Al-Khalidi, Mustafa. (1973). *Al-Tashir wa al-Istimar fi al-Bilad al-Arabiya*, Aladdin Printing and Publishing Company, Beirut, 5th edition,

Given the deep history of this endeavor—both the distant past and the recent history—along with the current situation, it is difficult for one to imagine the possibility of a fruitful dialogue for peaceful coexistence between the Christian and Islamic communities.

## 3.4.4 THE CONSEQUENCES OF THESE DIFFICULTIES AND THE PROPOSED SOLUTIONS:

The result of the difficulties arising from past actions has been the abandonment of any notion of rapprochement or alignment regarding the so-called "Abrahamic Project." This has been especially true for the Islamic side, which remains cautious about the other party, leading to strained relations and the failure of all efforts aimed at rebuilding strong ties.

Sheikh Muhammad al-Ghazali, in his reflection on the failure of attempts to reconcile, attributes this to their ill-timing, occurring at a moment when the wounds of the past had not yet healed. He states: "In this grim horizon, the idea of Christian-Islamic cooperation emerged. The idea, despite its nobility and goodness, is clouded with perplexing questions, if not outright disbelief. What does the hitter seek from the struck? Why approach him and take his arm? Where are they headed, and what are they carrying with them? Did the oppressor withdraw his hand, heal his wounds, and then come back to start a new plan based on forgiveness, cooperation, and mutual respect? No, none of that has happened."[124]

Al-Ghazali continues, emphasizing that the unjust political circumstances still choke the Muslims, threatening to suffocate them. How can there be friendship in such a situation? How can we expect affection from a relationship where the bonds have already been weakened? He argues that it is an insult to his dignity and a discredit to his moral and material senses to see Christian West strike him with

---

(pp. 34, 35).
124   Al-Ghazali, Muhammad (1411H-1991), *Kifah Deen*, Wahba Library, Cairo, 5th edition, (pp. 24, 25).

cruelty and savagery and then expect him to become a loyal ally, eager to support them.

This, he asserts, is the natural result of any unjust action and any oppressive treatment. The wounds of the past continue to haunt and alienate every effort at meeting, understanding, and reconciling. Despite numerous attempts at Islamic-Christian rapprochement in various capitals under the umbrella of the Abrahamic Project—conferences, seminars, workshops, and joint meetings—these dialogues have addressed important issues, most of which were chosen by the Christian side. Yet, these discussions have failed to meet the expectations that both sides had placed upon them, with the rapprochement project achieving none of its set goals.

Nevertheless, regardless of the goal or the outcome of these dialogues, the process of dialogue remains the most viable and successful way to convey the Islamic call to the people of the world, especially to Jews and Christians. This dialogue, in the form of *dawah*, contributes to overcoming the challenges and obstacles hindering rapprochement and mutual understanding. Only through mutual understanding and awareness of each other's perspectives can meaningful progress and reconciliation be achieved.

This writing outlines a few steps that could contribute to positive solutions for overcoming the difficulties that hinder meaningful dialogue, and for creating a religious dialogue environment in which the disputes and conflicts between the followers of the two religions are resolved—conflicts that seem to intensify with each passing day. These steps are as follows:

1. Christians must acknowledge that there were errors and crimes committed against Muslims in the past, and that these actions continue to be perpetrated against Muslims today across the world. Therefore, they must correct these mistakes and offer sincere and dedicated solutions to change the Islamic perception of Christians and those historical events. This would allow the pages of the past history to be closed.

2. The dialogue should be imbued with a religious perspective because religion is the primary and ultimate factor in uniting nations and peoples of different beliefs, religions, cultures, and civilizations. Religion determines the nature and quality of relationships with the West or others. As Huntington states: "Religion completely and sharply distinguishes between people; one can be half-French and half-Arab, a citizen of two countries at once, but it is entirely impossible to be half-Catholic and half-Muslim."[125]

Indeed, religion is the dividing line between people, and it also shapes the quality of their relationships with each other, both positively and negatively. This stands in stark contrast to what Edward, the U.S. Assistant Secretary of State for Near Eastern and South Asian Affairs under the Clinton administration, said in a famous speech in Washington, known as the "Merdian" media speech, where he claimed: "Religion is not a decisive criterion, whether negatively or positively, in determining the nature or type of our relationship with other countries."[126]

No, religion is a decisive factor. The course of the relationship between the West and Muslims was altered only by religion. The successive campaigns launched by the West against Islam were solely motivated by religious concerns.

For this reason, any rapprochement project must start from a religious foundation, and religion must be considered a central factor. The lack of understanding about religious issues has only expanded the divide, overshadowing other cultural, economic, and military attempts at cooperation. Therefore, religious issues must serve as the starting point for dialogue, from which its aims, goals, and broader dimensions can be explored.

As Sheikh Ahmad Deedat states: "If we look at all the dialogues between Muslims and Christians, we will not find this approach that God has commanded us to follow. Dialogue should focus on religion and monotheism... I wonder, what are they talking about? Oil prices, the status

---

125  Clash of civilizations, 16
126  Ibid., P.83

of women, the issue of slavery—has it ended or is it still present? God has taught us how to begin the dialogue with them, and we must follow His guidance."[127]

1. The parties involved in this religious dialogue and rapprochement should be the religious leaders from both faiths. This would ensure that the dialogue maintains a religious character, focusing on the fundamental doctrinal issues in both religions, which lay the groundwork for addressing the issue of global peace. Dialogue should take place between the religious authorities on the religious matters that form the core of mutual understanding, followed by other areas where experts in the political, economic, and cultural fields can participate. To claim that dialogue should encompass all aspects of life with the West is logically untenable. Such an approach lacks the necessary methodological accuracy and scientific objectivity. The relationship between Muslims—who are a collective body united by their belief in Islam, their shared heritage, and the true religion that forms them into a single Ummah—and the West, which is a complex and interconnected civilization driven by its own values, principles, ideologies, and policies, is not simply a matter of dialogue. The West is characterized by its movements and interests, which prioritize the preservation and expansion of its own values, pursuing these goals at the expense of others.[128]

2. The Christian side must acknowledge that there have been distortions and alterations in the holy scriptures, making them subject to containing beliefs and doctrines that contradict the core Islamic tenet of monotheism. This recognition is essential to open the space for meaningful dialogue and to create a common ground for both faith communities.

---

127  Al-Balag. (1989, 13/4/1409 AH). Issue 981, (p. 17).

128  Al-Tuwaijri, Abdulaziz bin Othman. (1418H-1997M). *Mustaqbal Afaq al-Hewar Bayn al-Muslimeen wal-Gharb*, Publications of the Islamic Educational, Scientific, and Cultural Organization (ISESCO), First Edition, (p. 8).

3. Missionary campaigns driven by Western colonial influence must cease, and the West should not impose its control, values, or principles on Islamic societies.

## 3.5 THE POSITION OF FOLLOWERS OF ISLAM AND CHRISTIANITY ON CORRECTING PAST MISTAKES:

### 3.5.1 THE CHRISTIAN PERSPECTIVE:

In his address at the Islamic-Christian Dialogue Seminar in Tripoli, Libya, in 1976, Christian interlocutor Father Jacques Langri suggests that the most suitable approach to correcting past mistakes and removing prejudices that have fostered distrust is as follows:

1. Acknowledge and repent for past mistakes.

2. Assess the present prejudices and the causes of misunderstandings.

3. Make efforts to alleviate and eliminate these misunderstandings.

4. Approach God with sacrifices and prayers so that the other party may feel and comprehend them fully.[129]

Father Kabouk, in a press interview with the Lebanese newspaper *Urban*, stated: "The past is gone, whatever it was. Let us place it in the archive and write a new history together, where brotherhood replaces conflict, and love replaces indifference. Come and see, for we have rebuilt our home."[130]

In this context, the Vatican Council's call encourages Christians and Muslims to forget the past and engage in mutual understanding, despite the many conflicts that have arisen throughout history.

Father Jacques emphasizes: "...that Christianity and Islam should build their relationship on a spirit of love, kindness, and empathy, excluding

---

129  Buḥūth wa Wathā'iq Nadwat al-Ḥiwār al-Islāmī al-Masīḥī. (1981m). Ṭarāblus: 2-6 Ṣafar 1396h – 1-5 Fibrāyer 1976m (§373, 374).

130  Ibid., p. 374

any other consideration... to eliminate prejudices and reduce the causes of misunderstandings that are causing significant harm today."[131]

Norman Daniel states: "To reach mutual understanding, we must not forget the past, as it remains a major obstacle to the dialogue process... If we are to start a new chapter in our relationship with Muslims, we must acknowledge our past actions and the mistakes we made against Muslims."

## 3.5.2 THE ISLAMIC PERSPECTIVE:

In his speech at the Islamic-Christian Dialogue Conference in Tripoli, the Muslim interlocutor, Muhammad al-Aishoubi, states: "The removal of erroneous preconceptions reveals to us the path of sound reasoning, and trust is fostered between us once we remove these biases. But can mutual trust have awareness, substance, and continuity if it is not accompanied by joint actions? What could be a better act than volunteering for the cause of justice among people and serving the oppressed peoples of the world? Our disputes, which date back centuries and stem from the ancient clash between the East and the West, will only cease when we all rid ourselves of a world founded on relationships of control and human exploitation, which have given rise to a crisis not of raw materials, but of humanity, its character, and its ethics. Religions must mobilize a force capable of ensuring peace and justice among people worldwide. This includes mobilizing all peoples and awakening global awareness to correct the horrific errors that threaten humanity. The true power of struggle and resistance lies in the will of the faithful, and the oppressed peoples who have overcome adversity have proven this."[132]

The Muslim interlocutor emphasizes the importance of removing preconceptions through the following steps:

---

131 Ibid., p. 373, also see, Secretariat Pro-non-Christians. (1981m). "Guidelines for a Dialogue Between Muslims & Christians." Edizion Ancora, Roma, pp. 73-105.

132 Buḥūth wa Wathā'iq Nadwat al-Ḥiwār al-Islāmī al-Masīḥī. (1981m). Ṭarāblus: 2-6 Ṣafar 1396h – 1-5 Fibrāyer 1976m (364

1.  Condemnation of the Crusades by the Vatican, which helps to uproot erroneous preconceptions in people's minds.

2.  A declaration that Zionism is a foreign element to Palestine and to the entire region of the East.

3.  A global campaign to work towards the return of Palestinians to their homeland, so that a Palestinian state can be established where Muslims, Christians, and Jews can live together, because only by returning the Palestinians to their homeland can a just and lasting peace be achieved.

4.  Acknowledgement that the issue of holy sites can only be discussed with the democratic Palestinian state after peace has been solidified, and that any efforts by organizations regarding the holy sites are considered grave injustices.

5.  Advocacy for UNESCO to issue an international charter guaranteeing every nation's right to technological and scientific progress, and this charter should be adopted by the United Nations. The technologically advanced world should not withhold the secrets of discoveries derived from profits gained from the Third World. The transfer of technological discoveries should prevent a potential divide between the Third World and the developed world. By eliminating political and economic injustices, we can create a world where humanity as a whole thrives, and cultures and civilizations are harmonized in a way that fully embodies human development.[133]

The Islamic perspective on how to eliminate preconceptions does not only focus on past events that caused these biases but also on the consequences and effects that followed, which have led to a persistent misunderstanding that hinders the process of dialogue, understanding, and rapprochement between the followers of the Abrahamic faiths.

---

133  Ibid., p. 365-366

# 4.0 CONCLUSION OF THE STUDY

Praise be to Allah, and peace and blessings be upon His Messenger. After this:

The results highlighted in this paper are as follows:

- It appears that the Abrahamic Dialogue project between Judaism, Christianity, and Islam raises numerous issues related to religious identity and doctrinal particularities. The attempt to unify the Abrahamic faiths within a single framework faces obstacles tied to religious pluralism, in addition to the political dimensions associated with the initiative. Despite the stated intentions to promote peaceful coexistence, concerns persist regarding the potential risks of erasing religious distinctions.

- There is a conflation between the concept of interfaith dialogue, which Islam advocates for, and the politically-driven Abrahamic project, which could lead to the dilution of the Muslim identity.

- The project is beset by significant challenges and obstacles, which seem insurmountable without abandoning the initiative altogether.

- The project has disrupted the healthy atmosphere of interfaith dialogue among the three Abrahamic religions.

- Abandoning the project entirely does not imply renouncing peace and peaceful coexistence.

# 5.0 RECOMMENDATIONS

- Conduct studies and write research and academic theses in Arabic addressing the Abrahamic project to raise awareness of its dangers to faith and the Islamic existence.

- Establish specialized centers to monitor and study this project.

- Enrich Islamic libraries with resources that strengthen this specialized area of study.

- Issue non-politicized fatwas regarding the risks of this issue, to preserve faith and maintain peaceful coexistence with others.

- Dialogue should focus on the foundational doctrines that Islam advocates, while steering clear of other agenda-driven topics such as economics and technology, due to the imbalance of power and equality between the parties.

- The study of controversial religious topics should be left to experts who possess the necessary knowledge of their aspects and complexities.

# 6.0 REFERENCES

## REFERENCES IN ARABIC

- "Al-Ahram al-Misriyya. (2000m, 21 February)."

- "Al-Ghazali, Muhammad. (1990m). Al-Taa'sub wa al-Tasamuh bayn al-Masihiyya wa al-Islam. Cairo: Ihsan Printing Press, Kuwait: Dar al-Bayan."

- "Al-Ghazali, Muhammad. (1991m). Kifah Din. Waha Library, Cairo, Fifth Edition."

- "Al-Haddad, (1969m). Madkhal ila al-Hiwār al-Islāmī al-Masīḥī. Al-Bulistiyya Press."

- "Al-Hourani, Abdullah. (Safar 1416h, Issue 185, Fourteenth Year). Al-Hiwār al-Nāfiʿ bayn Ashāb al-Sharā'iʿ. Daʿwat al-Haqq."

- "Al-Khalidi, Salah. (1995m). Haqā'iq Qur'āniyya hawl al-Qadiyya al-Filastīniyya (Second Edition). Muslim Palestine Publications, London."

- "Al-Shāhid, Muhammad. (1994m). Hiwar al-Masīḥīyya wa al-Islām fi al-Tawhīd wa al-Nubuwwa wa al-Qur'ān. A Critical Analytical Study of Hans Kung and Joseph Van Es's Views. Beirut: University Publications for Studies, Distribution."

- "Al-Shuwaʿīr, Muhammad bin Saʿd. (d.t). Wa Lan Tarda ʿAnka al-Yahūd wa La al-Nasārā. Al-Buhuth al Islāmīyya Magazine, Issue (33)."

- "Al-Tahāwī, Ahmad. (2002m). Tafsir al-Baghawī, Maʿālim al-Tanzīl. Dar al-Kutub al-ʿIlmīya."

- "Al-Tawbah, Ghāzī. (1998m). Bayn al-Hamalāt al-Ṣalībīyya wa al-Ḥurūb al-Yahūdīya – Muqārana wa Natā'ij. Al-Mujtama' Magazine, Issue 1300, (22-28 Muharram 1419h - 19-25 May 1998m), Year 29."

- "Al-Qaradawi, Yusuf. (1971m). Dars al-Nakba al-Thāniya: Limādhā Inhamnā.. Wa Kayfa Nantaṣir. Beirut: Dar al-Fikr, Second Edition."

- "Al-Qur'ān al-Karīm."

- "Durant, W. (d.t). Qissat al-Ḥaḍārah al-Sharq al-Adnā. Translated by Muhammad Badr."

- "Jaroudi, Rojīh. (1986m). Hiwar al-Ḥaḍārāt. Ouyadat Publications, Beirut: Third Edition."

- "Hayyāt al-Mūrīsikīyīn al-Andalusīyīn. Antonio Domingo Hortes. (1988m). Tarīkh Muslimī al-Andalus 'al-Muriskiyyīn' Ḥayāt wa Mā'asāh Aqlīyah. Translated by Abdul-'Āl Ṣāliḥ, Preface and Completion by Muhammad Muḥyi al-Dīn al-'Asfar."

- "İbn Hishām, (1955m). Al-Sīrah al-Nabawīyah (Second Edition). Mustafa al-Bābī al-Ḥalabī Press."

- "İbn Kathīr, Abū al-Fidā' al-Ḥāfiẓ Ibn Kathīr al-Dimashqī. (1987m). Al-Bidāyah wa al-Nihāyah. Edited by Dr. Ahmad Abū Malḥam, Dr. 'Alī Najīb 'Aṭwī, and Mr. Fu'ād al-Sayyid, Mr. Nāṣir al-Dīn. Lebanon: Beirut: Dar al-Kutub al-'Ilmīyah."

- "Sūsa, Aḥmad. (1972m). Mafṣal al-'Arab wa al-Yahūd fi al-Tārīkh. Baghdad, Iraq: Ministry of Information Publications."

- "Sūsa, Aḥmad. (1972m). Mafṣal al-'Arab wa al-Yahūd fi al-Tārīkh (p. 366, 367)."

- "The Holy Bible: Old Testament 1995 (Second Edition, Fourth Print); New Testament 1993 (Fourth Edition, Thirtieth Print). Issued by the Bible Society in the Middle East."

- "Zāwīd, Muhammad. (d.t). Al-Hawā al-Ma'ārifīyah."

## REFERENCES IN ENGLISH

- "Al-Faruqi, Ismail Raja. (1991m). Trialogue of the Abrahamic Faiths. International Institute of Islamic Thoughts, Herndon, Virginia, USA."

- "Blau, Joseph L. (1964m). Modern Varieties of Judaism. Lectures on the History of Religions sponsored by the American Council of Learned Societies. Columbia University Press."

- "O'Dea, Janet K., O'Dea, Thomas F., Adams, Charles J. Religion and Man-Judaism, Christianity, and Islam. Harper & Row Publications."

- "Secretariat Pro-non-Christian. (1969). Guideline for a Dialogue Between Muslims and Christians. Roma: Edizion Ancora."

- "Sidiqi, Ataullah. (1996m). Christian-Muslim Dialogue Problems and Challenges. Encounters, Journal of Intercultural Perspectives."

## ONLINE REFERENCES

- "Al-Qāsim, Khalid bin Abd Allah. (d.t). Al-Hiwār maʿ Ahl al-Kitāb. Muslim Library. [https://www.muslim-library.com/arabic](https://www.muslim-library.com/arabic)."

- **Huntington, Samuel P.** "The Clash of Civilizations?" *Foreign Affairs*, Summer 1993, vol. 72, no. 3, pp. 22-49. *GRIP*, 1993, www.grip.org/wp-content/uploads/2003/05/THE-CLASH-OF-CIVILIZATIONS_1993_Huntington.pdf

9 788826 936776